Growing as a Prophetic Singer

Anna Blanc

Growing as a Prophetic Singer
Copyright © 2013 Anna Blanc
annablanc.com

Published through Blanc Media
Editor: Edie Mourey (furrowpress.com)
Cover: David Carey (dcdstudio.com)
Interior: Dale Jimmo

Printed in the United States of America
ISBN 978-0-9896054-0-3

Thank you, Shawn.

You are God's greatest gift to me. Your steady, happy heart and willingness to step out into new things in obedience to God provoke me. You always know when to call me to rise up and not give in and when to encourage me to let things go. No one knows me like you do, and you love me like Jesus. You are my best friend, and I love you.

Thank you, Julie.

Your continual encouragement and timely corrections have saved my heart in different seasons. You are a mama to so many songbirds, and you are one of God's most valuable gifts to this singer community. Never stop telling your story and giving singers the strength to not quit.

Thank you, Paula.

Your willingness to yoke yourself to an insecure, beginning singer and pull her up into strength is truly rare. You are the most generous woman I know. I want a front row seat when Jesus shows you the vast influence you have had in the prayer movement all over the earth, one prophetic singer at a time.

Thank you, Justin.

You took a great risk in taking me under your wing. You were never hesitant to push me to the front and have stood confidently by, helping me find my way as a worship leader. Thank you for your patient instruction, constant encouragement, and friendship.

Contents

Foreword

In 1983, the Lord spoke clearly to us about starting a prayer ministry that would continue twenty-four hours a day, seven days a week. He spoke of it as "prayer in the spirit of the tabernacle of David." We understood this to be prayer that is led by singers and musicians. After all, the tabernacle that King David established in Jerusalem set a precedent of night-and-day worship. In fact, King David provided financially for 4,000 musicians and 288 singers to minister to the Lord night and day as their full-time occupation (1 Chr. 9:33; 16:37; 23:5; 25:7). He even commanded the future kings of Israel to uphold the worship ministry in the tabernacle with full-time singers and musicians (2 Chr. 29:25; 35:4, 15; Ezra 3:10; Neh. 12:45).

In 1999, we began 24/7 prayer and worship ministry in the spirit of David's tabernacle. By the grace of God, we have not stopped offering continuous worship and prayer, or intercessory worship, as we call it. It is the model we have used at the International House of Prayer of Kansas City (IHOPKC). It combines music, singing, and intercession to create an atmosphere for enjoyable prayer (Isa. 56:7). Musicians, intercessors, worship leaders, and singers all play a vital role in sustaining night-and-day prayer in our prayer room.

At IHOPKC, we have hundreds of prophetic singers on about twenty-five full-time worship teams. All across the earth, congregations and houses of prayer like ours are being blessed by prophetic singers and musicians. Singing is one of the most beautiful ways to declare the truth about Jesus. It is also powerful in times of intercession. The Lord Himself is a singer, and He sings over us (Zeph. 3:17).

I have been encouraging singers to sing prophetically for over thirty years. Singers and musicians must face and overcome specific challenges to grow in this grace. In different seasons of their ministry, they each face rejection, promotion, demotion, the need to grow in their skill, the need to study the Word, and much more.

Anna Blanc is one of our most faithful prophetic singers and worship leaders. Over and over again, I have watched Anna navigate the good and difficult seasons of her life as a singer and worship leader. I have witnessed her growth in maturity and wisdom. I have seen her become more adept at connecting with Jesus in both good and hard times. In other words, she has written this book out of the deep well of personal experience as a singer. She excels in this gift and lives a godly life of prayer with humility. She definitely backs up what she sings.

Anna has been on full-time staff at IHOPKC since 2005. She is also a teacher at our IHOPU Forerunner Music Academy, where she teaches an advanced prophetic singing class. Even during her college years before coming to us, Anna was a worship leader.

I am glad Anna has written *Growing as a Prophetic Singer*. It is definitely a book that has been a long time coming in that it has been so needed for those involved in intercessory worship.

Growing as a Prophetic Singer is a resource to help others learn practical skills as well as how to navigate the heart values, relational struggles, and other emotional highs and lows that accompany being a prophetic singer.

It is also helpful for worship leaders, musicians, and those who pastor singers and musicians. Regardless of the size or frequency of your worship services or prayer meetings, the issues addressed in *Growing as a Prophetic Singer* are common to all singers. It is a must-read for all singers, musicians, and worship leaders.

Mike Bickle
Kansas City, 2013

Mike Bickle is the director of IHOPKC, an evangelical missions organization based on 24/7 prayer with worship, combining 24/7 prayers for justice with 24/7 works of justice.

1

Using this Book

Prophetic singing is not for the faint of heart. I realize this more and more as I enjoy the pleasure of talking with singers in my ministry travels or as I participate in the International House of Prayer of Kansas City (IHOPKC) community.

In these conversations, other singers and I inevitably find ourselves discussing the glories and pitfalls of the journey of prophetic singing. Amazingly, in nearly every conversation, a singer will share how he or she feels isolated, disheartened, or challenged at some level. We seem to face some of the very same issues, like the pain of being so hidden, the toil of the mundane, the temptation to compare ourselves with others, pride, demotion, fear, etc. Our circumstances may vary, but the root struggles we face are the same.

In my years of prophetic singing, I have been through

many ups and downs. I have done well in some seasons and blundered my way through others. The testimonies of those who have walked this path and know well the way of the singer have buoyed my heart in times of trouble. In gleaning from the stories of those who have gone before, there has been one stabilizing factor, one constant. It both astonished and comforted my heart when I discovered it. I share it with you now to encourage you, no matter where you are in your journey as a singer in the Church: *you are not alone.*

You are not the first to taste the thrill of standing in worship as a vessel of the Lord. Neither are you the first to feel as though you can barely keep your head above the flood of discouragement that seems to rush in from every side. I now understand we all have experiences like these.

I was not born a naturally strong singer or confident leader. Each step of the journey for me has been a learned one. This is not how I would have written my story. I have often wished I did not have to work so hard in order to grow. I have wondered why the Lord has called me to function full-time as a prophetic singer without naturally equipping me with a high level of ability. However, I now look at the process of growing and stretching the Lord set me on as His kindness. And I am honored to have seen many of the angles of prophetic singing. I consider it my joy to look into the teary eyes of discouraged singers or feel the rush of the mountaintop zeal of those brand new to the calling, encouraging them all in their next step forward.

Please hear my heart. I do not mean to convey that I have some sort of fortitude in and of myself to share. On the contrary, I have seen the callow weakness of my own heart and abilities and have had to lean on the experienced coaching of those who have gone before me. I have asked the hard questions, made wrong decisions, and had to maneuver, in the grace of God, back to the path of faithfulness in the calling. The guidance and lessons I have gleaned are what I hope to impart to you in this book.

ANOINTING, EXCELLENCE, ENDURANCE

Put in the simplest terms, the role of the prophetic singer is what I call "the reach" for anointing and excellence with endurance. Reaching for the *anointing* as a singer is the reach for the presence of God and the spirit of prophecy in worship. We long for the Lord's presence and the spirit of prophecy that we may appropriately minister to His heart and the hearts of His people. The reach for *excellence* is an issue of stewardship; it is our faithful pursuit of the next ability level so that we may be increasingly effective messengers and see Jesus glorified. *Endurance* is the empowerment to persevere in every season— it is the strength not to quit, no matter what. With anointing, excellence, and endurance, the prophetic singer is equipped to ride the waves of adversity, stay faithful in the secret place of the heart in times of favor, and bring great glory to the Lord all along the way.

Each chapter in this book addresses an aspect of at least one of these three components. I have included practical help on how to grow in ability *(the reach for excellence)*. I cover foundational instruction on how to grow in the Word, develop language, and demystify what it is to prophesy as a singer *(the reach for anointing)*. Because, as I said earlier, prophetic singing is not for the faint of heart, I have included several chapters that are devoted to topics related to persevering *(developing endurance)*.

I have found that the heart issues like pride, envy, and the fear of man have the greatest potential to cut short the fruitfulness of a prophetic singer, not to mention the enemy's own devices meant to do the same. In exposing the things that may derail singers and in unveiling some of the truths of what the Lord sees in us, my aim is twofold: to both encourage and strengthen you. I have sought to be vulnerable with you about what I have been through in each of these subjects in hopes that you will learn from my failures and feel empowered by my breakthroughs in the midst of my weakness.

The exception to this pattern of topical instruction is the chapter immediately following this introduction: "Possessing a Biblical Vision for Prophetic Singing." A guide for prophetic singers would be remiss without laying out the broad vision in God's heart for music and singing in the earth. He is filled with zeal that His name would be praised in heaven and earth. The reason why any singer should bother to persevere at all finds its roots in His passionate plan for songs to arise worldwide. In the following chapter, I take the opportunity to paint the big picture of why we do what we do. It is from this perspective that we will zoom into the narrow focus of the remaining chapters.

CHAPTER TOPICS

In no way is this book comprehensive. Each chapter could easily be fleshed out into an entire book itself. I have not sought to cover the topics here in such a complete and exhaustive way. Rather, I attempt to provide a concentrated, approachable resource for prophetic singers in any setting, whether in a full-time prayer ministry or on a weekly church worship team. This book is meant to be a reference that can be returned to for insight and encouragement as the prophetic singer makes his or her way along the journey of our calling.

Because of this, I strongly encourage you to initially read the book in its entirety. Then it can be drawn upon topically in the future as you find yourself in one particular season or struggle. Though they strategically weave together in telling the story of a singer, each chapter can stand alone as a help in a particular area.

I do not take lightly the privilege to speak into your life as a prophetic singer. The Lord is intimately crafting your journey, and I am humbled to partner with His work in you. I count it a great honor to stand alongside you as a fellow singer. Each voice is valuable and necessary, and together we form a resplendent choir of praise to Jesus. He is worth our individually plunging wholeheartedly into our calling as prophetic singers. He is the reason for it all—He is worthy.

2

Possessing a Biblical Vision for
Prophetic Singing

There is something about music that deeply moves the heart of God. As the only being who could actually *choose* the circumstances surrounding His existence, He commissioned four living creatures to sing night and day before His throne without end (Rev. 4:8). Many times, at the climax of activity on earth or in the heavens, He ordained that the angels should break into song, ten thousand times ten thousand voices in great harmonies of praise (Rev. 5:11–12). He created all things, and by His *will* they exist (Rev. 4:11). This includes the very atmosphere surrounding His throne. God chose to dwell in the midst of singing because He *enjoys* it.

Because we are made in His image, the human spirit is musical and responds in deeply complex ways to song. Sometimes melodies have arisen as a reaction to powerful events. In Exodus 14, the Lord split the Red Sea, allowing the

Israelites to cross on dry ground as they escaped the Egyptian army. When they reached the other side and saw the mighty work the Lord had done, they lifted up their voices and sang what is referred to as the "Song of Moses" (Ex. 15; Rev. 15:3). Other times songs are actually ushering in the events of history, as we see in Jeremiah 31:7–8. Here the nations are exhorted to, "Sing with gladness for Jacob . . . proclaim, give praise, and say, 'O Lord, save Your people, the remnant of Israel!'" (v. 7). In the very next verse we see the effect this song will have as the Lord responds by gathering the people of Israel from the ends of the earth. Indeed, songs have shifted cultures and unified nations. This has given rise to the cross-cultural tradition of national anthems. Songs have confounded enemies (2 Chr. 20:22) and defiled generations. We still see the effects of the "sex, drugs, and rock 'n' roll" era of the 1960s which introduced a new level of immorality and licentiousness to American culture.

Inherent in a simple melody is the power to move the emotions of mankind to joy, laughter, tears, or despair. With the great influence God has given music to carry, it is no wonder He has woven songs into the fabric of His story that is being played out upon the earth as He makes Himself known through the generations.

AS IT IS IN HEAVEN

When Jesus' disciples asked Him for a lesson on prayer, He instructed them to pray, "Our Father in heaven, hallowed be Your name. Your kingdom come. Your will be done on earth as it is in heaven" (Lk. 11:2). This is to be the crux of our intercession and ambition in life: that His will would be brought forth upon the earth as it is, even now, in heaven.

In Revelation 4 and 5, we are offered an invaluable glimpse into the throne room of God. As we see what goes on around and before Him, we gain understanding into His will for the earth. There is nothing in heaven that is not in agreement with His desire. Every action, every spoken word, every sound is a great unveiling of God Himself.

As we look through the apostle John's eyes in the Revelation 4 scene of heaven opened up before him, we see a throne with a burning, radiant One seated on it (vv. 2–3). Amid the rolling thunder and voices surrounding Him are seven lamps of fire, the seven spirits of God in blazing glory (v. 5). In this terrifying beauty, we find the four living creatures in rapt attention. They are created to do two things: *gaze* and *proclaim*. As if to emphasize this point, God formed them with eyes all over their bodies, around and within. Under and around each of their six wings, these beings are *full* of eyes (v. 8). Two eyes would surely not have been enough. To blink and miss even a *moment* of seeing the radiating, beautiful One on the throne would be inconceivable for these four. And as their eyes unceasingly behold, the sight compels their proclamation: "Holy, holy, holy, Lord God Almighty, who was and is and is to come!" (v. 8). Over and over and over again, day and night without rest, they give glory and honor and thanks unending.

More than a description of the activity surrounding the Lord in heaven, this scene is an invitation to all who have ears to hear. The two activities of the living creatures—their gazing and proclaiming—beckon us to peer into the beauty and majesty of the One we love and declare His holiness in continual worship. *Especially* for us called to minister before the Lord as singers, our occupation must primarily be one of beholding. We must mine the Scriptures to know Him more fully and thus love Him more deeply. We must take the time to linger on descriptions of His nature and attributes of His person, letting the Holy Spirit breathe upon our hearts the awe and devotion He is due. Only then can we open our mouths and truly join the song of the four living creatures about the One seated on high.

THE TABERNACLE OF DAVID

Long before Jesus instructed us to pray that the Father's will be done on earth as it is in heaven, the Lord mandated "copies" and "shadows" of His heavenly temple to be established on the earth. God instructed Moses to build a tabernacle "according to the *pattern* which was shown [him] on the mountain" (Ex. 25:40, emphasis added). Moses' tabernacle was operating in the same vein as the Lord's heavenly place of habitation, as the Lord revealed it.

The Lord also gave David plans for a tabernacle on the earth, a place where the Lord's glory would dwell among His people (1 Chr. 28:11, 19). In this later revelation of God's desire for a dwelling place, the Lord gave instruction for music to arise before Him day and night as a sacrifice of praise. David financed 288 singers (1 Chr. 25:7) and 4,000 musicians (1 Chr. 23:5) to function in the tabernacle of the Lord. He also instructed the leaders of Israel in coming generations to continue the tabernacle of worship the way the Lord had revealed it to him (2 Chr. 29:25; 35:4, 15).

The Lord's decree for worship to go forth in the place where His presence will dwell among His people on earth reveals His intention for the unceasing praise that takes place in heaven to be mirrored on the earth. He desires the praise and petitions of the saints to rise as incense (Rev. 5:8). As it is written: "'For from the rising of the sun, even to its going down, My name shall be great among the Gentiles; in every place incense shall be offered to My name . . . for My name shall be great among the nations,' says the Lord of hosts" (Mal. 1:11).

HIS WORTH

When first confronted with the Lord's intention for unceasing praise in heaven and on earth, we must ask the question, "Why?" Why all the trouble and organization that undoubtedly went into Israel's government-funded tabernacle of praise? With over four thousand musicians and singers, it is clear that considerable energy and resources went into maintaining the order and livelihood of these worship teams. Even today, with so much work to be done for the kingdom of God on the earth and so many people to be reached with the gospel, why should we take the time and effort to lift our voices in worship? Taken a step further, why would God *call* and *appoint* some to be singers, whether full-time or for a few hours a week, to minister before Him? Isn't there a far better use of time, energy, and resources?

The answer is simple, yet one that spans from the reason behind creation itself to the purpose of the dawning of each new day: His infinite worth. When we have experienced but a taste of His grandeur and glory, the only legitimate response is abandoned worship. The twenty-four elders who cry out before His throne say it this way: "You are worthy, O Lord, to receive glory and honor and power; for You created all things, and by Your will they exist and were created" (Rev. 4:11). And the apostle Paul said it another way: "For of Him and through Him and to Him are all things, to whom be glory forever" (Rom. 11:36). We exist *for Him*.

There are many ministry assignments, callings, and positions to which the Lord will appoint His people for the sake of His kingdom, but the primary assignment for each person to whom He gives breath on the earth is to *behold* Him and *adore* Him.

THE CRY FOR JUSTICE

Acutely related to our role of adoration in response to the worth of Jesus is the cry for justice. As our hearts are fixed on seeing Him lauded on the earth just as He is in heaven, the many inconsistencies between the two locations become glaringly apparent.

The truth is, spiritual darkness pervades the earth. Men reject God and cling to unrighteousness, feeding their hearts on sin in self-gratification and falling far short of the glory of God. Though injustice has many faces—the oppression of the poor, the murder of babies in the womb, the enslavement of women and children—its chief expression is in the heart that refuses to repent and glorify Christ. Thus, the apex of injustice, and the root of all other injustice, is that the worth of Christ is unrecognized and men's hearts are unresponsive to His glory.

As believers who adore Jesus foremost, we are driven to cry out for justice upon the earth—that He may receive the praise of which He alone is worthy. Fleshed out, this looks like intercession for the salvation of souls. It includes the feeding of the poor, freedom for the captives who are bound, and protection for the weak and vulnerable. These prayers and acts are birthed not out of altruistic motives by humanitarian effort, but rather from a place of zeal for the name of Jesus. We long that He be seen and magnified in every place and His light break into every darkness.

Speaking of the Father's exaltation of Jesus, the writer of Hebrews says, "He put all in subjection under him, He left nothing that is not put under him. But now we do *not yet* see all things put under him" (Heb. 2:8, emphasis added). This phrase, "not yet," should quicken a longing, even an ache, within us as we see that all things are not as they should be. He is not lifted up in all things, and men continue to use the very breath He supplies day by day to turn and curse Him, their Maker.

As ones who love His name, a cry wells up from within us, "Oh God! Have mercy and save souls!" We long that all who oppose Him would come to love Him and that He should receive the adoration of yet another life of which He is worthy.

THE ROLE OF SINGERS

Though the Lord has made each human heart to lift up its voice to Him in song, He has specifically assigned some to function in the role of a prophetic singer. The Lord has made a way for many to minister before Him on a full-time basis. In locations throughout the earth, this is becoming more and more common. For others, they have felt the call as singers and are serving in part-time capacity in their communities, either on a church worship team or on a few sets in their local house of prayer meetings.

Just as in Israel with David's tabernacle, the Lord is setting singers in place throughout the nations of the earth who continually bring before Him a sacrifice of praise and call forth His purposes for justice in the earth. These prophetic singers are charged to minister before Him, "to commemorate, to thank, and to praise the Lord God of Israel" (1 Chr. 16:4).

Singers are called to a place of leadership in the Body of Christ. We lead others in song so that all may gather and worship Him. Whether for a congregation of three believers or three hundred thousand, we are commissioned to faithfully direct the gaze of the Bride to the Bridegroom and lead her in offering up the songs of her heart to His. The Lord also releases songs through us that are based in His Word. These songs we sing over His people that they may be strengthened in Him.

It is remarkable how our hearts are knit to the Lord's purposes as we sing such songs. As prophetic singers, we not only lead others in adoring Jesus, but we assist them in joining their hearts to the cry for justice upon the earth. Music and singing make intercession sustainable over longer periods of time, and they make prayer more enjoyable.

UNTO HIS RETURN

While we will see breakthroughs and waves of revival as we stand in intercession and praise, things on the earth will not be as they should until the day of His coming. We are not merely content to worship the One we love as He is seated in the heavenlies or make requests of Him whom we have yet to see. Rather, the fulfillment of our every hope is found in the day He splits the sky and we are with him face to face. Jesus Himself *is* justice, and He is the One we long for as we join the song of the Spirit: "Come, Lord Jesus!" (Rev. 22:17).

Isaiah prophesies of a day when a new song will arise from the ends of the earth. Those who dwell in the cities, islands, coastlands, wilderness areas, and mountaintops will join in high praise as the Holy Spirit orchestrates worship in every place (Isa. 42:10–12). As songs in every language and tongue mingle and ascend before His throne, the Lord will stir up His zeal like a mighty man and prevail over His enemies, returning to the cries of His Bride (Isa. 42:13–16). The coinciding events of intercession from the earth and the return of the Lord are evident in heaven in Revelation 5:8. As the bowls of incense, which are the prayers of the saints, become full, Jesus steps forth and takes the scroll from the hand of the Father. This begins the judgments immediately preceding His return.

With the songs of the earth rising alongside the coming of Jesus as King, it is no surprise that the enemy comes in with a flood of lies and snares to keep prophetic singers silent. Over the years, I have seen singers taken out through the wiles of the enemy, and I have struggled myself to endure through the many trials that come. As we look through some of the issues and glories of prophetic singing, may we reach for anointing and excellence with endurance.

3

Countering Comparison, Envy, and Pride

The enemy actively and consistently seeks to introduce comparison, envy, and pride to the hearts of prophetic singers. These noxious weeds start out subtly and grow just under the surface till they eventually choke the callings and anointing of God in us. Of course, these are issues every person faces, no matter the calling. For singers and musicians, however, these three temptations are elevated to another level.

The reason for this greater intensity level is that, unique to singers and musicians, our abilities can be measured fairly easily just by our listening. We can tell within minutes if we are better or worse than another singer. An evaluation of another's and of our own excellence can be made fairly quickly; whereas, other areas of gifting are a bit more hidden and difficult to analyze.

Show an average person two rocket scientists, for example, and he will have difficulty finding who is more capable in their field. Have the two rocket scientists sing, on the other hand, and the person can readily judge which scientist has the best voice. Because our voices are so vulnerable to immediate evaluations like these, our hearts really have to battle to stay free from comparison, envy, and pride.

COMPARISON

Since evaluation of singers comes so easily, the natural outflow of this for our sinful flesh is to compare ourselves with others. Most often, comparison is the poisonous weed that takes out brand new singers. In fact, both envy and pride find their roots in comparison. When we compare ourselves with another and feel less gifted, we slip into envy. When we feel more able than another singer, we find ourselves in pride (though there are many other faces of pride as well).

No good thing comes from the practice of comparison. What farmer is constantly comparing the young sprout he just planted with the mature, fruitful vines and measuring its height against them? Our Vinedresser does not pit us against one another, and we should follow His lead.

I once had a friend quit serving as a singer, explaining there were so many gifted singers at IHOPKC that she thought she should just let *them* minister as prophetic singers. I believe this way of thinking grieves the heart of God.

When forming the specific natural abilities and potential for growth in an individual, the Lord is intentional. He is not random in the way He distributes all varying levels of talent to different singers. I like to picture prophetic singers as clay vessels tenderly formed by the Potter. Each one is unique in appearance and function; no two are identical. Isaiah 64:8 paints this picture well, "But now, O Lord, You are our Father; we are the clay, and You are our potter; and all we are the work of Your hand."

I tremble to think of all the times I have pierced the heart of the great Artist by looking to another vessel and weighing my (and their) worth. I cringe when I think of the times I have accused Him of being unkind for calling me to be a singer but not giving me a high level of natural talent from birth. He is as purposeful with each and every prophetic singer as an artist with each piece he creates. The specifics of how we are made as ministers through singing and the details of our journey of growth are meant to just as purposefully bring glory back to Him.

BRINGING HIM GLORY THROUGH WEAKNESS AND STRENGTH

We often overlook the fact that we bring the Lord great glory when we operate at full capacity before Him in our calling, even when we are weak. I used to wonder, when I first started worship leading, why the Lord did not give me a voice that was naturally refined and powerful. I would see other singers around me who had never taken a lesson in their lives, and they had voices that could thunder over a room. The Lord began to reveal to me that He receives glory from each of us in varying ways. When I would give Him all my heart in a worship set, He was glorified before men by my obedience—even when I still had so much more to learn spiritually and vocally. Because I did not have the natural ability to stir a room simply through my gifting, I was *forced* to lean into the Lord. And in different sets when there would be a tangible breakthrough of His presence, I knew, my worship team knew, and the room knew it was of *Him*. In my beginning stages, it was clear I could not *make* anything happen; the glory could not be misdirected to me but belonged only to Him.

At the same time, when we *have* reached a level of personal excellence as singers, we glorify the Lord by operating in our full strength of ability while keeping our hearts and motives set on Him. It is rare for an individual who is rich in any realm of earthly power—whether it be money, intellect, or ability—to sustain a heart of humility and service to the Lord. It is extremely glorifying to the Lord when a prophetic singer with a high level of excellence loves Him with the whole of his or her gifting, using this strength to usher others into adoring Him.

STOP IT, STOP IT, STOP IT!

About a year ago, the Lord confronted me once again regarding the presence of comparison in my heart. I thought I had largely dealt with this issue. For my first three years at IHOPKC, I had tried to sound like someone I was not. It seemed so powerful to me when other singers would belt out loudly in their low range. I wanted this to be my primary expression of singing, too. This was a terrible goal for me as a soprano with a more naturally classical voice. In the end, I just sounded mediocre.

Through the wisdom and unrelenting encouragement of my voice teacher, I began to make peace with the sound of my voice. I began to sing like *me* and not like others I was trying to imitate. Interestingly, as I worked at expanding my range and singing classically on my own, my voice began to grow in versatility as well. Some of the sounds I reached so hard for in the beginning started to come more easily as I threw my energy into expanding the abilities that came naturally to *my* voice.

However, on this occasion the Lord kindly revealed that I was not through with the snare of comparison. I had just finished singing a main IHOPKC Friday night service with my worship team. Julie Meyer, a prophetic woman and friend the Lord has used many times to encourage and correct me, was the worship leader. In our post-set debriefing, Julie turned to me and pointed her finger at me, saying, "Anna, the Lord says, 'Stop it, stop it, stop it!' Stop comparing yourself with other singers. Your voice is *unique*, and you need to *thank* Him that your voice is different than everyone else's."

As she spoke, I felt the Holy Spirit moving on my heart. This was truly what the Lord was speaking to me. I had "made peace" with my voice and accepted that it was different than I had initially hoped, only it had never occurred to me to *thank* the Lord for making my voice the way it is. And I realized then that, honestly, I *wasn't* grateful. Still, deep inside I wished I had been given a different voice.

As I left the parking lot that night, I began to speak out in gratitude, even though I did not feel it. I began to thank God for giving me a more classical sound. I thanked Him that I was a soprano. I thanked Him that my voice was unique from the ones I had envied all this time.

As the minutes went by, my heart began to shift. It was as if my spirit had been stiff and sore for years and was finally free. The ice that encased the statements I was making before the Lord was beginning to melt, and my gratitude began to take on real meaning. I really *was* grateful. I really *did* like my voice. He gave it to me this way, in His perfect wisdom, and I was thankful.

THE POWER OF GRATITUDE

Psalm 100:4 encourages us to "enter into His gates with thanksgiving, and into His courts with praise," and 1 Thessalonians 5:18 instructs us, "In everything give thanks; for this is the will of God in Christ Jesus for you." There is a reason why the Lord so often in Scripture commands us to give thanks. Gratitude is the number one spiritual combatant against bitterness and anger. A thankful spirit naturally uproots and prevents dark emotions from poisoning the soil of our spirits. It is impossible to be truly thankful before the Lord for our gifting while simultaneously envious of what He has given another.

When we set our hearts to be grateful to the Lord, we must also let go of self-pity, self-centeredness, and anger. In fact, we can test our hearts to see if we are cultivating these sinful tendencies by how genuinely we can thank Him for what we have been given. As soon as my heart hesitates at truly thanking Him, I know I have harbored the roots of envy and pride within. At this discovery, the enemy will also seek to introduce shame at my having failed to keep a pure heart. Do not give him a further foothold by allowing yourself to enter the self-imposed prison of condemnation. This is entirely fruitless for the kingdom and not of God.

Instead, as soon as you see comparison, envy, and pride in your heart, confess them to the Lord as sin. Repent sincerely, and you will be *immediately* forgiven. There is no delay, no penalty period—you are pure! Begin to speak again the words of thanksgiving to the Lord. It is through repentance and confession of the truth that your heart will gain freedom. Continuing in a lifestyle of gratefulness before the Lord as a prophetic singer is the best safeguard against an offended, envious heart.

PRIDE: THINKING TOO LOWLY

Pride is a difficult topic to tackle because of its many faces and vast influence on the human spirit. There are different forms of pride we struggle with as prophetic singers. Pride, in its core, is thinking higher or lower of ourselves than God thinks of us. Humility is agreeing at the heart level with God's opinion of us.

Oftentimes, we overlook the fact that a low opinion of ourselves is an expression of pride. I believe the Lord wants to shine His light on this underestimated seed of sin; it is one so commonly given over to in the lives of prophetic singers. When we claim a lower value of ourselves than Jesus gives us, then we are saying, in essence, that we know better than He does.

I remember my first year of singing. I would come back to the briefing room after sets for the post-set meeting, and the first thing out of my mouth would be what a bad job I had done. Maybe it was that I was off pitch during a song, or I missed a cue from the worship leader, or I sang something really silly that had come out wrong. I just *had* to let everyone know. We all do this; I've seen it over and over again on a near daily basis through the years. What I was *really* saying when I wanted to talk about my weakness in front of everyone was that I wanted everyone to know that *I* knew that I had messed up. I was just *sure* that everyone was thinking about how off pitch I had sung, so if I let them know that I was aware of it too, at least they wouldn't think I was an idiot! The root of these negative admissions was concern over how I was perceived by others.

As soon as I began to realize what I was *truly* saying, I was struck with the amount of pride hidden behind that seemingly harmless practice of self-negativity. I immediately purposed before the Lord that, without explaining to anyone what I was doing, I would keep silent after a set about my performance, *no matter what.* This vow I have kept to this day. I haven't done it perfectly, but very rarely over the years have I diverted from this commitment. What I have found is that this silence works a deep, even excruciating, humility in my heart. It is painful! I have sung some pretty amazingly weird things, and to not give the qualifier afterward in front of the team dug deeply into my pride. To come back after an off day of struggling with pitch and not say, "Wow, I sounded terrible today," injured my pride. It killed the part of me that wanted everyone to know that I knew I was off. I was so concerned that others would think it was how I normally sounded!

Bearing that stigma without qualifying myself began to teach my heart to live before the eyes of the Lord in a deeper way. Even if my singing during a set permanently affected my worship leader's opinion of me, *just one glance* from the eyes of the Lord could release immeasurable power upon my singing. In choosing to not constantly voice my weakness, I was leaving my reputation in the hands of the Lord alone.

PRIDE: THINKING TOO HIGHLY

As the more common expression of pride, we can all identify with thinking too highly of ourselves. This is what we typically think of when we are addressing pride.

Harboring the pride of high-thinking in our hearts is actually a lack of love for others. This is what Paul was addressing when he said, "Let nothing be done through selfish ambition or conceit, but in lowliness of mind let each esteem others better than himself. Let each of you look out not only for his own interests, but also for the interests of others" (Phil. 2:3–4). Instead of assuming our own greatness and seeking our own gain in regard to our reputation, we are to bolster others in their callings. When we spend our strength in an effort to help the advancement of another, we are working in the opposite spirit of pride and ambition.

What we do *not* want to fall into when addressing this sin is self-abasement. This is simply falling into the rut on the other side of the road, and it is still pride. The balance I believe God is looking for is that we would see ourselves as great, but understand *why* we are great.

All the boastful statements you could make about yourself fall far short of the high praise the Lord gives for those who love Him. In the Song of Solomon, the Beloved (who can be understood to be the Lord) says of the Shulamite (who represents believers, His Bride), "O my love, you are . . . lovely as Jerusalem [the city He cherishes], awesome as an army with banners" (6:4). In Ephesians 5:25 we see that Jesus "nourishes and cherishes" us as His Bride. We are His treasure! In John 15:9, Jesus tells us that He loves us with the same quality, amount, and intensity of love with which His own Father loves

Him. This is an astounding truth about our value to God.

The reason we are so great is because *we are His.* Our success is rooted in Him alone. We are beautiful and glorious in His eyes because He has desired us from before the foundation of the earth, and He has clothed us in His own righteousness. Something is only worth what someone is willing to pay for it, and our worth is boundless because He gave *everything* to have us. He ascribes to us our value; without Him, we are nothing. The moment we begin to find any amount of worth in ourselves apart from Christ, we are in selfish pride. We can boast in Christ *alone.*

4

Remaining Faithful in Hiddenness

The truth is that the whole of our lives are lived and worked out in hiddenness. It does not matter if you are a rock star worship leader in a megachurch or the nameless and faceless singer on row thirty. If you love Jesus, then who you really are is a great secret that is hidden away in Christ.

It may seem in this age as if image is everything. Sometimes it may even feel as though the more people who know your name, come to your worship sets, and tell you how gifted you are, the better life is. Even in the Church, we tend to exalt personalities and value what will draw a crowd, but the truth is that these things are all a smokescreen. They are a brief flash of beauty that is here today and gone tomorrow, quickly fading away. God does not see as man sees, and He has a very different opinion.

Through one simple directive, Jesus shocked the religious

leaders of His day who were operating in the natural human tendency to loudly display their piety and obedience to God before men. He said, "When you pray, go into your room, and when you have shut your door, pray to your Father who is in the secret place; and your Father who sees in secret will reward you openly" (Mt. 6:6).

Your Father *who is in the secret place*. How many times have we declared and sung to Him that wherever He is, that is where we want to be? However, we walk through our days, filling our schedules, stomachs, and homes with as much as possible, even with legitimate labor for the kingdom. We cast furtive glances toward the stillness and aloneness of the secret place, knowing that we *should* voluntarily seek Him in hiddenness, but the fear of barrenness and boredom convinces us to continue in our busyness.

This statement from Jesus, that the Father is in the secret place, should cause us to shake off our apathy and contentment with our frenzied existence and come away with Him in new measure. He is waiting for us in that place. If the worst of our fears becomes reality—we willingly seek Him in the secret places of our lives and feel bored and empty—*still we have been with Him.* His eyes behold the one who comes away in secret, and He receives every moment as love, regardless of what we feel we have received from the experience (as though we could even begin to measure the deep workings of the Lord within the human heart).

34

The great Writer of history has determined that this age will culminate in the most surprising plot twist known to man. When Jesus returns to the earth, He will turn the world as we know it on its head. The value system of man will be seen as worthless foolishness, and things done in secret, both bad and good, will be clearly evident to all. On that day, the wisdom of obedience in the hidden places of life will be justified. There will be many believers sorrowful on the Day of Judgment because the things they gave their lives to will be burned up when tested by fire (1 Cor. 3:13–15). In His kindness, He has told us this beforehand.

We are all called to separate ourselves to the Lord through time spent with Him alone. This is the ultimate *secret place* of our lives where we meet with God. But even beyond this voluntary coming away, there are three main areas of hiddenness I believe we will be held accountable for before the Lord: the hidden places of circumstance, motivation, and the thought life. Each requires diligence and watchfulness that we may be found faithful in every way when we stand before the Lord. And as we sincerely seek Him in each of these hidden places of life, we stumble upon a great gift in that *we find communion with Him.*

THE HIDDEN PLACE OF CIRCUMSTANCE

Our circumstances are always changing. One minute we are in a place of prominence before men, and the next we are at the back of the line. Julie Meyer calls these ups and downs in circumstances the "Ferris wheel of favor." Seasons of promotion and demotion are common to all, but for singers it feels as if these seasons shift more frequently and with greater extremes, as if the Ferris wheel of favor travels around double speed. We will address many of the particulars of these seasons in the coming chapters entitled, "Developing through Demotion" and "Passing the Test of Promotion." Our perspective on the shifting of circumstance will be dramatically affected by how we set our hearts to live faithfully in hiddenness.

When you are in a season where the Lord has moved you into a role that is more hidden from the eyes of man, where the impact is largely unnoticed, you face a struggle to maintain a thankful and faithful heart. We naturally want to be noticed by others with our ministries having a big, measurable effect. Instead, when we are serving in a less-appreciated role, we are faced with the challenge to still serve well and to the fullness of our ability. Though no man may notice or care, the eyes of the Lord are fixed upon our hearts, *especially* when we are overlooked by others. We are to serve others in secret, knowing that we are actually serving the Lord Jesus. As it says in Scripture, "And whatever you do, do it heartily, as to the Lord and not to men, knowing that from the Lord you will receive the reward of the inheritance; for you serve the Lord Christ" (Col. 3:23–24).

The vast majority of prophetic singers and worship leaders

called by the Lord to minister before Him will be in a hidden place of circumstance. Most houses of prayer and churches that the Lord is raising up all over the earth are relatively small in attendance and perceived influence, yet mighty in spirit and entirely necessary to the Body of Christ. It is a delusion to think that, if you are called by God to minister as a singer, your ministry will be very public and valued by many. This misconception is dismantled when things do not grow bigger and better. When this happens, many quit and assume they missed the call of the Lord over their lives.

I want to be very clear that the majority of singers called and appointed to lift their voices to the Lord, declaring Him faithful and calling for His return, will be stationed in small, even remote, gatherings throughout the earth. But it is in the perceived smallness that you will find this glorious reality: the Lord is there in your midst day by day. He is with you in secret; stay faithful.

FAITHFULNESS IS HIDDEN

We are so quick to look at the more visible, platform ministry singers and be in awe of their level of ability. We look with the eyes of men, seeing the external evidences of greatness, and we laud these ones. We rejoice in their gifting and praise their success. This is not necessarily a bad thing; it is what comes naturally to us as human listeners. It actually is good to affirm singers who are serving the Lord. What we usually fail to notice is that for every visibly successful singer there are ten who are laboring just as hard in their calling as prophetic singers in less noticeable roles. While the eyes of men are drawn to one group of singers and just as easily overlook another, the eyes of the Lord see something entirely different.

In 1 Samuel 16, the prophet Samuel is standing before the sons of Jesse, preparing to anoint the next king of Israel. As he sees the oldest son, he becomes confident this is the one chosen by God. In that moment, the Lord startles him, saying, "The Lord does not see as man sees; for man looks at the outward appearance but the Lord looks at the heart" (v. 7). One by one, each of the impressive-looking seven sons passes by Samuel, but the Lord does not approve of any of them as king. Finally, the youngest son, David, is brought in from his labor of keeping the sheep. As he stands before Samuel, the Lord says, "Arise, anoint him; for this is the one!" (v. 12). The one chosen and anointed by God to rule over the nation of Israel was the one overlooked and forgotten even by his own family. But God knew him well.

Talent does not wow God, and crowds do not move Him. Likewise, the ones who have lesser natural abilities do not escape His vigilant attention. His eyes are fixed intently upon the hearts of all men. What He is looking for—what actually moves that great, burning heart—is *faithfulness*. David was a young, under appreciated boy who kept sheep, alone in a field. He spent his days singing songs to God with no one around to even hear him. Yet something about David's unwavering faithfulness to serve well and love God no matter what caught the Lord's gaze. When those eyes of fire discover a heart that is fully set to love Him through wholehearted obedience, no matter their station or ranking, He is *moved*.

The way that faithfulness is so entirely hidden in this age is a grand set up by the Lord to rightly evaluate and order the age to come. Let's pretend for a moment that there are ten levels of singing ability, one being the least and ten the greatest. One particular singer may be naturally gifted at a level two and be largely overlooked by man. This singer may be locked into the gaze of the Lord, undeterred by the oversight of man. He may continue in faithfulness in his calling as unto the Lord, taking lessons and increasing in ability over time. After several years, this singer may double his abilities, landing at a level four. However, the eyes of man notice and praise the level five and above singers. This prophetic singer will *never* attain a big platform, never influence the multitudes, never be affirmed by a crowd. But the eyes of the Lord will have seen *every moment* of faithfulness and dedication. His unswerving devotion to obedience and excellence in his calling will have caught the eyes of the coming King, and he will be *greatly* rewarded on the day he stands before Him.

In contrast, another singer may have been born a level six singer, immediately catching the attention of man. She may never do what it takes to increase her skill or set her heart to sing *only* because of the eyes of the Lord. She may coast along for years, never knowing that the Lord actually gave her the ability to sing at a level eight if she would only apply herself in diligent practice. The Lord absolutely still loves this singer and will reward her for the ways she did serve faithfully, but she will miss out on the fullness of reward He wanted to give her had she pressed in faithfully to apply herself wholeheartedly.

HE SEES IN SECRET

The most explicit display of the Father's eyes taking note of our lives as we live them out in hiddenness is at the baptism of Jesus. In that point of His life, Jesus had not begun His public ministry. He was not known as the Great Healer or Deliverer; He was not sought out as Teacher or Miracle Worker. To the eyewitnesses of His baptism, Jesus was merely a thirty-year-old carpenter's son from Nazareth. But at the moment Jesus came up out of the water, the Father thundered over Him from heaven, "You are My beloved Son, in whom I am well pleased" (Mk. 1:10–11).

Well pleased. Before the miracles, before the crowds and inception of His ministry, the Father's evaluation of His Son's life left Him *well pleased.* This should stir our hearts to see that every seemingly insignificant moment in our mundane, routine lives is lived out before the attentive eyes of the Father. He takes note of every action, thought, and attitude of the heart lived out in secret. Each moment is an opportunity to love and delight Him as we live for His eyes alone.

One evening four years ago, during the last week in December, I was standing on the main stage preparing to sing at IHOPKC's onething conference. The multicolored stage lights were set, fog machines pumped out their mystical haze, and a sea of chairs stretched out before me. I watched as thousands upon thousands of young people rushed through the doors, hoping to get as close to the stage as possible. As the lights began to dim in the room and the musicians began the first few chords for worship, I closed my eyes. Instantly, a picture flashed before me. I saw myself earlier that day, sitting at my piano in my bedroom, singing before the Lord. No one had known or cared what I was doing in that moment hours earlier; I was completely alone. As this scene came before me, I heard the Lord whisper, "Anna, I see you the same."

The same. Spotlights and microphones do not impress Him; He is looking at the heart. I had equal opportunity to touch God sitting in my room, singing Him songs, as I did on a stage in front of twenty thousand people.

Oh that we would not discount the small, the unnoticed, and the weak circumstances while singing before Him. We care so much about impact and influence, and for what? If we were to capture the attention of one million people in a day, we would still be simply forgotten by them a month later. Let us never get so wrapped up in counting the pairs of eyes upon us that we miss the only gaze that really matters. He sees, and that is all that matters in the end.

THE HIDDEN PLACE OF MOTIVATION

Motivation—the very intent of our heart—fuels everything we do as prophetic singers. Behind all our actions, both good and bad, is a motivation. We can even do the *right* thing for the *wrong* reason or the *wrong* thing for the *right* reason. While our actions do matter, the Lord is equally concerned with the motivation of our hearts that bring those actions to pass.

Paul exhorts us, "Therefore, whether you eat or drink, or whatever you do, do all to the glory of God" (1 Cor. 10:31). The motivating factor behind each decision we make should be that God would be glorified. It is very sobering to think that I can outwardly appear to be in perfect obedience and labor for the Lord but internally be motivated by pride and selfish ambition. This thought provokes the fear of the Lord in me. Man may pat me on the back in celebration of my actions, but God's eyes are piercing into the hidden place of my motivations. He cannot be fooled.

As I begin worship sets, especially when the external circumstances are not ideal or there is a heightened temptation to "perform" before the people in the room, I try to focus my heart on the Lord in a clear way for those first few minutes. I whisper phrases to Him, expressing that the intentions of my heart are set on His glory in the worship set. I ask Him for help in the areas where I need a realigning of my motivations. Sometimes even opening up the Bible to a verse in the Psalms that expresses the beauty and greatness of God helps to keep my heart motivated for the purpose of His worth and glory.

THE HIDDEN PLACE OF THE THOUGHT LIFE

No matter how hard we may try, we cannot stop thinking. Though our mouths may be silent, there is constant activity going on internally. As singers, our thoughts can be so quick to stray from the Lord as we sing the same familiar songs and passages we have led a hundred times. With no warning, our thoughts can begin to drift, and before we even notice it, we are thinking about what we are going to have for lunch, or recalling the details of a conversation we had earlier in the day. Even in these harmless "bunny trails" of thinking, we want to train our minds to be fixed upon the Word and the Lord at all times—especially when we are ministering before Him.

We have a phrase here at IHOPKC that "just past boredom is revelation." Though you have sung a certain passage of Scripture for the last ten weeks or you have worshiped to a particular song for years, choose again to engage your mind with the Holy Spirit. It is in the moments we least expect that a nugget of deeper understanding is dropped into our spirits.

Another struggle common to prophetic singers in the area of the thought life is the temptation to think negatively or critically while singing. We can slip so easily into evaluating ourselves and the other singers on our team, or we can get annoyed that the worship leader is leading a particular song we don't like. Maybe the worship leader cut you off while singing ten times during the set already, and you are tempted to become frustrated. How quickly we can go from a critical spirit into anger and offense. As soon as we recognize that our thoughts are straying into negativity, we must repent and refocus our minds upon the Lord. Again and again, even hundreds of times a set, we must bring our minds back before Him. We must offer our hearts and thoughts to Him, asking, "What are You saying, Holy Spirit? What are You doing in this prayer meeting?" The remarkable thing is that as we take the time to set our minds on Him and ask, He will speak to us and lead us as we sing.

If we take the time to posture our hearts before Him, we will see that the Holy Spirit is waiting for us in the secret places of our thoughts—that every thought can be in conversation with Him and be well-pleasing to Him. The constant working of our minds that we so often take for granted is a vast, opportune place to meet with and love the One our hearts desire.

5

Developing through Demotion

It does not matter how humble, mature, or seasoned you are; demotion always bears a sting. Whether it comes when someone else takes your leadership role, when you are let go from your worship team, or when you are a worship leader and your whole team quits in one week, demotion is a fiery affliction that the Lord brings in His perfect timing. This season change often comes as a direct answer to our cries to Him of, "Lord, make me more like You."

Challenging our motivations and shaking the foundations of our identities, demotion exposes our hearts in ways few other seasons can. In the midst of demotion, our hearts are laid bare before us, and we see grime, chaff, and darkness rise up in what we thought were our pure and dedicated hearts. What we often overlook is the fact that being demoted did not cause sinfulness to arise in our hearts; it simply *revealed* what was already brewing within. The Lord will often use seasons of demotion to bring to our attention what has been before His eyes all along. To the sincere heart, this is a priceless gift.

DEMOTION IS FROM THE LORD

One absolute necessity during these seasons of difficulty is to understand that your leaders who are imposing the demotion are not the ones who are shifting your season. It is not by chance, human decision, or a random series of events that you are losing your current position or perceived favor; it is the hand of the Lord who is changing your circumstances. This understanding can initially add more pain to an already difficult situation. There is at least a morsel of comfort in self-pity when you feel simply overlooked by man, and there is some satisfaction in self-righteous anger if you sense an ambitious spirit in the one taking your place. But if *God* is the one behind this demotion? Ouch!

"Is He unkind? Am I in some massive, unperceived sin? Does He love that person more than me?" These are the types of questions that rock our world. But don't shrink back in some expression of fake submission to His "unknowable, mysterious will"—enter the wrestling match! Ask the hard questions. Let that sting be productive in opening your heart to the Lord. At the bottom of every sincere, difficult question is the gold of the knowledge of God.

Five years ago, I was a primary singer on a worship team.

All at once, three of the most talented and anointed singers at IHOPKC joined my worship team, and I found myself on the back row, sharing a microphone with two other singers and only permitted to sing on choruses. The pain of this demotion dug deeply, but I found comfort in shared experience with these two others on the team. Then, within three weeks of the initial demotion, the Lord moved them both on to primary singer roles on other worship teams, but He left me right where I was—alone.

I knew this was the Lord's doing. I *knew* it. My worship leaders had done nothing wrong, and the gifted singers who joined were divinely led to join the team, one even through a supernatural dream. God's hand was clearly at work—so why did He set me up for this? It felt mean and incredibly humiliating. Yes, He needed to deal with my pride, but wasn't there another, less public way?

Day after day, worship set after worship set, I would battle for my heart. Many times I could not even sing the choruses without being choked up with a swirl of emotion. Thankfully, my tears of frustration were mistaken by my team members for tears of tenderness at the beauty of the worship set! But inside, I felt like quitting every single day.

After several months, God used Julie Meyer to reach me in my pain. She has been through these seasons and is a "mom" to many at IHOPKC. She spoke the word of the Lord to me once again. She said, "Anna, the Lord is not punishing you by demoting you. *He wants you all to Himself right now.*"

From that moment on, it was as though a light had been shone into the darkness of my confusion. Slowly I began to see the thorns hedging me in as a tender space for me to give God my heart. I began to see how He *waits* in the secret place to meet with me (remember the Matthew 5 verse in the previous chapter). I went from feeling like an unwilling captive to savoring the time spent with Him alone on the back row. Yes, it was a difficult season of stepping back from ministering through interactively singing with a team, but I got *Him*! His invitation was not to stepping back and being alone; it was to stepping back and being *with Him*.

THE INVITATION TO COMMUNION

When the Lord's hand actively pushes you down in terms of external position, He is issuing you an invitation to communion. He is removing some of the peripheral busyness and distraction, and He is drawing you near. He is inviting you to the mat where wrestling results in the hard, deep, experiential knowledge of Him.

I think that when David wrote, "He makes me to lie down in green pastures," he was referring to this invitation in the midst of difficult circumstances (Ps. 23:2). He *makes* me lie down. He removes the options, sets His hand upon me, and takes me lower. However, the glorious reality is that, once our eyes are opened, we see that He has made us to lie in *green pastures*. There is great fruitfulness and satisfaction in this place. It is in the delay between feeling the force of His hand and the opening of our understanding that the true battle for righteousness takes place.

However distant I had felt from the Lord those first few months, He was unrelentingly engaging my heart. Those times I could not see or feel or understand Him were when He was most at work in me. I felt like quitting every single day, *but I didn't*. My eyes were blinded to it at the time, but my ability to endure and sing with a struggling but sincere heart was proof not of His absence, but His *nearness*. And though feeling every arrow and toil of the battle, I was successful because I did not give up.

REFINEMENT

The Lord uses demotion to refine us. As singers, we are mere vessels of varying kinds for His glory. Unfortunately, like everyone else who walks the earth, we have this propensity to draw attention to ourselves and find fulfillment in our roles as if they were our identities. Demotion is one way the Lord tests and exposes this in our hearts. The psalmist knew this when he wrote, "For You, O God, have tested us; *You have refined us as silver is refined.* You brought us into the net; You laid affliction on our backs . . . We went through fire and through water; but You brought us out to rich fulfillment" (Ps. 66:10–12, emphasis added).

Do you know how silver is refined? It is put through

intense, excruciating heat that causes all imperfections to burn away. There is a deep and intentional work the Lord is doing in the fiery affliction of demotion. Do not be thrown off when you see the sinfulness of your flesh rising to the surface. Though it may feel repulsive, this is a true gift from the Lord. He is committed to not leave us in our state of uncomfortable awareness of our sinful tendencies; He will wash them away as we stand before Him asking to be cleansed. This is His promise; He will finish the work He has started, and He will bring about rich fulfillment.

DO NOT CHANGE YOUR OWN SEASON

You can derail the purposes of the Lord in this season of your life. Though you *feel* captive in some circumstances, the Lord will never violate your free will. I believe many miss out on the depths of intimacy with His heart He longs to give simply because they refuse to stay in the battle during seasons of demotion.

The automatic reaction of the human heart when we feel pain is to stop the pain. This is no surprise, but it should put us on our guard when the pain we are feeling is the Lord's active leadership in maturing us. We can, if we are not discerning concerning His leadership in our lives, opt out of the very season He had purposed to grow us up into His likeness. When it is the Lord who has you in the lowest place, do not get up too quickly. James puts it this way, "Count it all joy when you fall into various trials, knowing that the testing of your faith produces patience. *But let patience have its perfect work,* that you may be perfect and complete, lacking nothing" (Jas. 1:2–4, emphasis added).

I encourage you to let patience have its perfect work. There is a real *work* the Lord is doing in the midst of the trial of demotion. While we are freaking out at and dealing with the vast amounts of pride and ambition we suddenly see within, He is active in the depths of our hearts, working His nature into us, that we may be perfect, complete, and lacking nothing. Now *that* is worth every ounce of pain. The Holy Spirit's plea is that we would agree with His leadership over us though we may not understand it, and that we would "let patience have its perfect work."

WHY DEMOTION?

Seasons of demotion are not always in response to glaring sin or pride. The Lord will sometimes demote the one whose heart is lifted up in pride or who is in blatant, known, unconfessed sin. Many times, though, the Lord is simply seeking to bring our lives to the next level of fruitfulness.

Jesus said, "I am the true vine, and My Father is the vinedresser. Every branch in Me that does not bear fruit He takes away; *and every branch that bears fruit He prunes, that it may bear more fruit*" (Jn. 15:1–2, emphasis added). I believe the Holy Spirit would say to many singers in a season of demotion, "You're doing well! You are bearing fruit." So many who name

His Name do not bear fruit, but you are faithfully remaining in Him. As the Overseer of your soul, He sees when you are to be taken to the next level of maturity for His namesake. Endure His pruning in the season of demotion, and you will be astounded at the fruit He will bring forth from your life. His leadership is perfect.

ON DISPLAY FOR HIS GLORY

Beyond the deep work the Lord is doing within us during demotion, He is at work in others through us. There is a typically unwelcome reality that when we are demoted it seems as though everyone is watching. The workings of God in our hearts, that we wish were private and unspoken, are shouted from the rooftop. Demotion as a singer just happens to be most often public, with everyone having a front row seat to your response. It is pertinent during this time to sign up once again to do all things before His eyes alone. And when we do, the Lord displays through us the beauty, transformation, and vast riches of His grace toward the one who waits on Him, even through pain—especially through pain! We have all been provoked to a deeper obedience and love when we see someone give glory and honor to the Lord through a difficult season. As you live before Him alone in the midst of trial and demotion as a singer, you are glorifying Jesus and drawing others to Him in a beautiful way.

How the Lord must trust us weak, fickle humans that

He would put us on display in the midst of our weakness. He is risking the glory of His name in highlighting us in our moments of trial and weakness. Feel His honor of you in the midst of demotion. He trusts you. He will never allow you to be tempted beyond what you can handle well to His glory. Lean into His strength, and say yes to Him again and again, day by day. He knows *just* what He's doing in you.

6

Passing the Test of Promotion

The Lord intentionally brings seasons of promotion in our lives. He is a brilliant leader in that He strategically shifts our circumstances at exactly the right time to simultaneously work righteousness *in* us and accomplish His purposes in others *through* us. In promotion, we become a more visible vessel of ministry to His people. Through this, He tests our hearts with the crucible of the praise and attention of man.

Oftentimes the Lord will bring a season of promotion just when we become comfortable with the previous season of lowliness. The Lord is not looking to increase our comfort but rather our righteousness, and He knows just the right circumstances to bring that will make us into His likeness. As in seasons of demotion, it is His hand bringing about the change in perceived favor. In the words of my singer friend, Lisa Gottshall, He is the "Master of the seasons, Ruler of the winds; the times and the storms still obey His commands."

A season of promotion can be expressed in different ways. Maybe you were asked to join your favorite worship team or were asked to be a head singer for the first time, or maybe you came up with the latest chorus that is being sung by all the other worship teams. I see promotion as any moment when we are given the call or opportunity to step forward as a singer. However it comes, we must never fall into the dangerous thought pattern that we have somehow earned or deserved the increase in favor. This sense of entitlement stems entirely from pride and is a seed of darkness the enemy would like to sow in our hearts. When it seems just the right people are noticing you and your gifting, it is important to realize that it is the Lord who is directing their eyes and not your abilities gaining their attention. Everything we have has been given us from the Lord.

The truth is, the season of promotion should cause us to tremble. We should be acutely aware of the potential temptations birthed in pride we will no doubt face. As circumstances change for the better, it is critical to remember we are being tested. Those burning eyes are looking past the externals, right into the inner man. This thought should ever grip us until we bow our hearts in humility to the One who weighs our every motive and intent. May our earnest desire be that He is pleased with what He sees in us.

WHY PROMOTION?

When we approach a season of promotion as not all fun and favor but as an actual test of the heart, we can begin to see its divine purpose beyond ourselves. The truth is, we are all merely little vessels walking around—vessels of His presence and glory—and conduits of His ministry. While He does use promotion to deeply work His nature and humility in us as we respond in a right way to His leadership, His first intention in promoting us is to bless His people through us.

In 1 Corinthians 12:4-7, Paul explains, "There are diversities of gifts, but the same Spirit. There are differences of ministries, but the same Lord . . . But the manifestation of the Spirit is given to each one *for the profit of all*" (emphasis added). As the Lord increases your gifting or gives you a greater ministry platform, it is for the profit of His Body. He desires to richly bless the congregation of saints, so He anoints His vessel (you) in a way that encourages, blesses, and edifies the whole. The increase is not primarily to benefit you; it is for *them*.

In this way, we can actively honor the Body of Christ by stepping forward to serve her in our elevated role during promotion. We can put on the meekness of Christ and love her by fully operating in our gifting. We can reach incessantly, every moment, for the word of the Lord, that we might sing His heart over His beloved ones. This takes hard work, time, and energy. Greater levels of influence carry with them greater burdens and responsibilities. By saying yes to the new level the Lord is inviting you into, you are committing your heart and resources to loving others as yourself.

Oftentimes in the Body of Christ, we take promotion and notable favor from God as the Lord's stamp of approval on an individual's character. We assume that if God is using someone to greatly impact others such a one must be humble, righteous, and full of truth. In actuality, the Lord's favor has less to do with the inner life of the vessel than we assume. The Lord raises up some and uses them powerfully in ministry though their hearts are ensnared along the way in ambition and pride. For sure, the Lord will judge wickedness in the hearts of these, but the time delay between the lifestyle of pride and the Lord's judgment is different for each of us. After all, He does show us mercy, even using the delay to provide us with opportunity to repent and be changed.

This truth, that the Lord uses His vessels primarily to bless His people, should also fill us with the fear of the Lord. When you notice you are in a season of promotion, it is essential to continue in vigilantly holding your heart before the Lord. Let your cry be: "Search me, O God, and know my heart; try me, and know my anxieties; and see if there is any wicked way in me, and lead me in the way everlasting" (Ps. 139:23–24).

Keep your heart open to the searching gaze of the Holy Spirit. More than promotion and favor, more than a platform or influence, we must deeply desire holiness in the innermost places of our hearts. When we stand before the Lord one day, we may be asked to give account for our influence on the lives of others but not for its size. God is not interested in how big our ministry has become. He is much more intimately interested in how we tended to the garden of our own hearts. And that is what He will hold us in high account for.

UNWELCOME PROMOTION

Not all times of promotion are welcome. I remember my first big promotion as a singer at IHOPKC. I had been singing for about a year, during which time I was usually one of the last singers on the line-up. I was new to singing and still figuring out how to hear notes to sing during antiphonal singing and still learning how to control my voice.

Suddenly, there was a mass exodus of singers from our worship team until there were only new beginning singers and me. By default, I became the main singer. I was terrified! I would get so nervous transitioning onto a set that I would lose feeling in my arms, and my hands would cramp. It felt so humiliating to be pushed to the front when I was not ready vocally. But the Lord was stretching and growing me, causing the new level of leadership and expectation to spur me to rise to the occasion. He was kindly leading me to step forward even when the shoes were too big for me to fill. I have learned this is all part of the Lord's process for growth.

If you are given a season of promotion when you do

not yet feel qualified, you must fight the temptation to back down. It can feel humiliating to step forward into a new level of leadership. You may feel as though it is clear to everyone that you are out of your league, and in some cases, you may be. This is one way the Lord continues to work humility into us at deep levels. Will you trust His leadership, say *yes*, and step forward though you do not feel ready?

FUNCTIONING AT FULL CAPACITY

Most of us are familiar with stepping back, making a way for others, and bowing low as an expression of humility. This is good and right. However, humility sometimes means stepping forward. We can hinder the work the Lord intends to do in us by constantly stepping back from the limelight in the name of "humility." Acting in humility requires we simply obey Him when He says to step up or step back. Our role in living humbly is to sustain a big, wholehearted *yes* to whatever the hand of the Lord is doing.

One way we express this yes to the Lord is by functioning at full capacity, no matter where we are put. Were you just demoted to the back row? Say yes to the Lord with your whole heart and sing with all your love and the best of your abilities. Were you just given more responsibility? Do not shrink back even if you do not feel ready. Open your heart to the Lord and step forward with the assurance that it is well pleasing to Him. Give Him your all by functioning at full capacity.

FAKING IT

When I first began to lead worship, I often felt as though I were faking confident leadership during the worship sets or in front of the worship team. Inside I felt insecure and unsure of my decisions, but because I was in a new level of leadership, I externally presented my thoughts and directions as if I knew exactly what I was doing. After conversations with several other worship leaders, I discovered I was not the only one feeling this.

While I knew that directing the team with confidence was best for everyone involved, I still felt conflicted at representing myself in the opposite spirit than what I was feeling within. *Am I being fake?* I remember thinking while in this dilemma. I specifically recall asking similar questions of the Lord one evening as I stood in front of the stove cooking dinner. Out of nowhere I heard that still quiet voice of the Lord speak into my being. He said, "Anna, you're not faking it—you are leaning into My strength."

The Lord's words shifted my thinking about this permanently. I'm not faking it; *I'm leaning into His strength.* I'm pulling from a confidence and strength of leadership that I do not possess in myself, but *He* does. He is a strong, sure, unwavering leader, and by His Spirit that lives in me, I too can function in strength and boldness. Do not give into the fear and insecurity you may feel at this point as a singer. Lean into the strength of the Lord and step out with confidence.

And so, we are equipped with greater skill and deeper love for others as we respond rightly to promotion as prophetic singers. Through His perfect leadership, Jesus is faithful to refine our hearts and teach us His way of servanthood in the position of leadership. Every season in Him is filled with purpose, and we can trust His wisdom every step of the way.

7

Facing Fear

If you have been a prophetic singer for longer than ten minutes, you have probably had to deal with fear. It may come as slight nervousness or full-on terror, depending on past experiences and your personality. Fear is a great challenge that all prophetic singers face and must overcome.

I do not believe you are ever entirely free of the battle with fear. It may continue to be a struggle in varying contexts throughout your journey as a prophetic singer, but you do not have to be ruled by it. Do not give into it and allow it a foothold, even for a season; we must constantly *participate* in the battle for freedom and boldness. The enemy will not back down from using fear in an attempt to stop us from fulfilling our calling, so we must never back down in claiming the grace and freedom available to us in Christ Jesus.

I have always loved the verse where Paul tells Timothy that we have not been given a spirit of fear. It was not until I had been a prophetic singer for several years, however, that I realized Paul was encouraging Timothy as he struggled with fear *in the midst of his ministry calling.*

Paul said, "Therefore I remind you to stir up the gift of God which is in you . . . for God has not given us a spirit of fear, but of power and love and of a sound mind. Therefore . . . share with me in the sufferings for the gospel" (2 Tim. 1:6–8). He was calling for young Timothy to not shrink back as he was assaulted from the enemy with fear. He was challenging Timothy, instead, to stir up, or draw upon, the gift of the Holy Spirit within him. From this place of dependence on the indwelling Spirit, Timothy was exhorted to operate in his ministry calling—to preach the gospel—without trepidation.

Like Timothy, we have to stir up the gift of God. We must learn to lean into the power of the Holy Spirit and step out in our calling as singers who prophesy.

FEAR IS FROM THE ENEMY

Fear is not from God. This may seem obvious, but if we understand this truth, then why do we cower under the power of fear? Everything that is from the enemy we are to resist and refuse (Jas. 4:7). He comes to steal, kill, and destroy (Jn. 10:10). He attempts to remove us from our calling to minister before the Lord as singers, and fear is one of his favorite weapons.

The initial effect of fear is that it causes us to feel *powerless.* We feel overwhelmed, weak, and unable to sing. However, the

Lord is actively working on our behalf in the opposite spirit. As we draw upon the power of the Holy Spirit within us, He is releasing to us a spirit of *power*, love, and a sound mind (2 Tim. 1:8).

I remember my first time traveling with the onething regional ministry team. I had only been singing for about a year, and I was asked to accompany the team as a singer because my husband was the drummer for the trip. I was gripped with fear during every worship time and even during the sound check! When it came time to sing antiphonally, I would shrink back. I hoped it was not obvious I was too afraid to participate. I thought it would be better for the stronger singers to carry it anyway; I was afraid that I would mess the whole thing up if I sang.

During one of the breaks between sessions, an experienced singer pulled me aside and gave me a word of advice. She said, *"Anna, timidity is not from the Lord."* The fear I had been giving into and even rationalizing was not from the Lord. It shook me up a bit to think that I had been giving such a foothold to the enemy in my heart.

I purposed right then that I would say yes to the Lord when He was making a way for me to step out in boldness. I have not done this perfectly by any means, but just having the commitment before the Lord to respond in the opposite spirit when I'm feeling fear has been massive in plumb-lining my heart again and again in truth.

SPIRIT OF FEAR

Prophetic singers can be assailed by an actual demonic spirit of fear. I don't believe it is a spiritual attack *every* time we get nervous when we are singing. There are many factors that can play into our emotions and nerves. However, when there is a sudden, seemingly out-of-proportion terror that grips our hearts out of nowhere, I have come to realize there is a good probability it is demonically driven.

The good news is that we do not have to succumb to the fear that seems to be entangling us. In fact, as disciples of Christ, we are given authority over a spirit of fear. Jesus said to those who follow Him, "I give you the authority to trample on serpents and scorpions, and over *all the power of the enemy*" (Lk. 10:19, emphasis added). Demonic spirits have to obey Jesus' authority, and He has commissioned us to use His authority.

It does not matter how weak you feel emotionally in the moment; the name of Jesus is all-powerful. As we speak out to bind a spirit of fear (or any tormenting spirit), our confidence is not in ourselves. Our confidence is securely in the victory of Jesus over the enemy. Colossians 2:15 says, "Having disarmed principalities and powers, He made a public spectacle of them, triumphing over them in it."

Satan has no legal right to afflict the people of God. And God has left to us the responsibility of enforcing His victory over the power of the enemy. We must do our part in standing in the victory Christ has already won. It is not enough to sit back and endure fear as a singer. We must rise up in our God-given authority and command fear to leave, knowing that "He who is in [us] is greater than he who is in the world" (1 Jn. 4:4). As in many areas of life in the kingdom, God is looking to partner with us.

In the moments when fear comes in like a flood, and it seems you can't find your way alone, ask a friend to partner with you in standing against the demonic attack. About a year ago, I had this happen in my own life. I found out on a Sunday that on Friday night I would be worship leading at the Awakening Service (a revival-type service that took place during the week). Though I had led worship in larger contexts several times before, this time I became gripped with terror.

From Sunday through Tuesday, I went through my days with thoughts of the three-hour worship set constantly before me, like a ticker tape in my mind. My heart rate was quicker, and I had a constant stomachache. I would lie awake at night for hours, unable to turn off my brain and fall asleep. Even though I would think things through and rationally see there was nothing to be so afraid of, I was still gripped with fear.

Finally, on Tuesday afternoon, I pulled Laura Hackett aside to pray with me. She had led these meetings continually for about a year, and I knew she had fought the battle of fear herself. I felt silly explaining how terrorized I was by the coming worship set, but it was all too real to me. I knew that even confessing my struggle with fear would help unlock my freedom.

Laura laid hands on me, and we began to agree for my freedom from the spirit of fear. About a minute into her prayer, I suddenly felt heat throughout my body, and I began to shake. It lasted only a few seconds, but I knew something powerful had taken place.

As soon as our time of prayer was over, I felt like a different person. Truly, my heart was still and my body at rest. No butterflies in my stomach, no freaked out heart rate. I felt peace for the first time in days. For the rest of the week, that peace rested on me just as strongly as the fear had previously. I slept well each night and felt a stillness in my inner man regarding the worship set I was to lead. I was still nervous when it came time to worship lead, but I was not gripped and overwhelmed with fear. The change in me was tremendous.

Do not bear the weight of dealing with a spirit of fear alone. Though you may feel nothing in the moment you pray together with another believer, much takes place in the spirit as we take authority over fear, and the enemy has to flee.

FEAR OF MAN

Another expression of fear in the life of a prophetic singer is the fear of man. This snare has many faces and is ever an issue from the time you are a beginner to when you are an experienced singer. The fear of man creeps into our steadfast dedication to please the heart of God and subtly shifts us till our end goal is to please others. Our eyes that were once locked with His piercing gaze lower until our constant concern is what others are thinking and how they are evaluating us.

When I first began to lead worship publicly at IHOPKC, I saw the fear of man in my heart in a way I had not been aware of. I had led a team for over a year in another context where we led worship week after week before an empty room. I remember the first time I led worship in the main prayer room that was full of people. As I left the stage, I suddenly felt *horrified* at what I had just done. I had opened up my heart before complete strangers. I had placed the strengths and weaknesses of my voice before them, opening myself up to praise and criticism and all the varying opinions of man. And in that moment, my heart was laid bare before me. Without realizing it, I had let the fear of man hijack my emotions and sway the purpose of my heart from worshiping before the eyes of One.

People have opinions. There is no way around it, and pretending that everyone is for you, thinking well of you, will never truly fool your heart. The truth is, there will always be a varying array of opinions swirling around you as a prophetic singer. One worship leader may like your style of folk singing; another may wish you sang more classically. One intercessor will tell you that you are her favorite prophetic singer while another thinks someone else should have your role as the chorus leader on the team.

There is no escaping the sea of public opinion about your performance as a prophetic singer. What takes the power out of that great, intimidating consciousness of external evaluation and steadies our hearts once again is the truth that the opinions of man *do not count* before God.

The one opinion that matters and the only correct evaluation of you is what the Lord thinks. He has made clear the standards He holds for us if we long to be pleasing in His sight. If we live sincerely reaching for holiness and humility, if we sing with our end goal being to bring Him pleasure and glory, then we are successful in His eyes. As simple as this may be to understand, it can become quite difficult to continually realign our hearts to focus on the One we seek to please.

Imperceptibly to me, my gaze will begin to wander in different seasons. At some point during a worship set, I will find myself wondering if a certain person in the room is thinking well of me, or pride will rise in my heart when I feel I have done well in a certain setting. I see in those moments that I have strayed from my first love. When we see that the sin of the fear of man has crept in, we must repent and recommit our hearts to fear the Lord only and worship Him.

Into the epic story of human history and eternity, God has woven the fabric of your life. Your song is a small piece of His vast strategy to raise up songs that usher in the second coming of Christ at the end of the age. Do not let anything—not sin, not intimidation, not fear—take you out of the grand story He is writing.

8

Knowing Three Truths

There is considerable emotional traffic that comes with being a singer. This is stirred up by the spiritual elements of warfare and the daily rigors of serving well in the midst of the mundane. Even if you are in a season where singing the Word each day as your vocation feels glorious, still the bills have to be paid, meals cooked, the lawn mowed. There are always the complex dynamics of dealing with others at work, in ministry, and at home.

I sometimes sit on the stage about to sing a two-hour set and feel as though I am wearing all the swirl of life's issues draped over my shoulders. Still at other times, after I settle in onstage to sing for the set, the Holy Spirit convicts me of something I did or said to someone earlier. I then repent to the Lord and receive His forgiveness, though I have to be a prophetic singer for *two hours* before I am able to contact the person I wronged.

Now *that* is a struggle against condemnation!

In all the internal battle in my calling as a prophetic singer, there are three truths that have kept me pressing in over the years. I have found that these stabilize and encourage me in and out of season. They are great antidotes to the poisonous lies the enemy uses in attempting to derail my heart from what the Lord has called me to do. I share them now, trusting they will do the same for you.

HE SEES

The first truth that sustains me is that every time we sing a worship set with a sincere heart of worship to the Lord, He receives it as love and is pleased. *Every time.* Even when our eyes are blinded to any form of impact, our offering of worship reaches His ears. Just the fact that we are coming again and not giving up is a gift of faithful love in His sight. If what we do is truly all about His receiving honor and pleasure from our song, then in this we can be confident that we are successful; not one moment or struggle is wasted when it is offered to Him in love.

In Revelation 5:8, we see that in heaven there are "golden bowls full of incense, which are the prayers of the saints." This is astounding. Our weak cries to the Lord actually appear before Him, in His very throne room. Our prayers, offered in utter weakness, are represented before God Himself with the tangible scent and form of incense filling real, physical bowls.

How we radically undervalue our prayers.

In the Old Testament, the Lord required the sacrifice of animals—that they be burnt on an altar. The smell of that sacrifice was pleasing to the Lord. Now we are commanded to "continually offer the sacrifice of praise to God, that is, the fruit of our lips, giving thanks to His name" (Heb. 13:15). The fruit of our lips—our words—are pleasing to the Lord and come before Him as a sacrifice, a demonstration of love. David says in Psalm 116:17, "I will offer You the sacrifice of thanksgiving, and will call upon the name of the Lord."

It could be said that the Lord is looking for *words*. The setting of our hearts in obedience and sincerity in our worship is key, but we must also speak and *sing* to Him. This is what delights His heart.

The next time your heart feels discouraged as you go to sing the same old songs and prayers, fix the eyes of your heart on the perspective of heaven. Know that this is not symbolic. Your voice is represented before Him literally; see your words to Him becoming real smoke, strong scent, before His throne, and see the way it touches His heart. This is why what we do actually matters—because it matters to *Him*.

OUR SINGING HAS POWER

Because we are so in touch with the weakness and mundaneness of what we do day after day, and because we routinely evaluate our productivity by what we have produced with our hands, it is easy to lose sight of what is truly happening in the spirit as we serve the Lord as singers. The second truth that sustains me is that though God is all-powerful and can move and shift things in the spirit without any help from us, He is profoundly relational and *chooses* to partner with us in releasing His power. This is an astounding reality; He forgoes the speed and ease of simply gaining the spiritual victory in every area immediately, though He is certainly more than able. Instead, He *waits* for little human vessels to come into agreement with His will and ask for Him to move on behalf of righteousness and justice.

As we take our place as prophetic singers in intercession, we are offering ourselves to the Lord as vehicles of releasing His will upon the earth. The Father has chosen intercession as the primary way He releases His power through us, and even more profoundly, through His own Son, Jesus. Hebrews 7:25 describes Jesus as the High Priest who "always lives to make intercession for [us]." Romans 8:34 explains, "It is Christ who died, and furthermore is also risen, who is even at the right hand of God, who also makes intercession for us." What an honor that God calls His Church to stand in the place of intercession, joining His very own Son in calling forth the things of His heart upon the earth. Whatever this beautiful Man is doing, that is what I want to be found giving myself to—that I may be *with Him*.

Intercession is speaking and singing God's heart back to Him. He has made His plans and purposes known to us in

His Word. We are to discern His will and call it forth in faith and partnership with Him, and He answers by stretching out His hand in authority. Jesus taught us to pray, "Your kingdom come. Your will be done on earth as it is in heaven" (Mt. 6:10). He calls believers into intercession saying, "The harvest truly is great, but the laborers are few; therefore pray the Lord of the harvest to send out laborers into His harvest" (Lk. 10:2).

Jesus taught that justice would be established through night-and-day prayer. Justice, put simply, is making wrong things right. The Lord's judgment against sickness is to bring healing. His judgment against the lies of the enemy that keep people bound is to bring freedom and salvation. Jesus is the ultimate social reformer and King of justice, and He connects social reform and justice to night-and-day prayer. He teaches, "Will not God bring about justice for His elect who cry to Him day and night, and will He delay long over them? I tell you that He will bring about justice for them quickly" (Lk. 18:7–8, NASB).

The power the Lord breathes into our declarations of His heart's desires is astounding. Singing simple prayers may not seem like much from our perspective, but the Lord is truly *listening* and *waiting* for the opportunity to accomplish His purposes behind those small, sincere cries. Misty Edwards, a senior worship leader at IHOPKC, says of this partnership between God and man, "Prayer is so simple that anyone can do it. But it is so simple that few actually do it." If only we had eyes to see what is taking place in the spirit as we lift our voices, we would be convinced there is no greater way to affect the earth for God's glory.

One of the most dynamic examples given in Scripture of the power of singing offered to and anointed by God is in 2 Chronicles 20:1–22. A great multitude of Moabites and Ammonites were moving toward Judah to destroy her, so King Jehoshaphat cried out to the Lord in desperation under the dire circumstances. The Lord spoke to him through a prophet. He was instructed to go down against the enemies the next day, though there would be no need to fight in the battle. The Lord would go before them, for this was His battle.

The next morning, Jehoshaphat "appointed those who should sing to the Lord, and who should praise the beauty of holiness, as they went out before the army and were saying, 'Praise the Lord, for His mercy endures forever.' Now when they began to sing and to praise, the Lord set ambushes against the people . . . who had come against Judah; and they were defeated" (2 Chr. 20:21–22). In the same way, as we go before the Lord with praise, He moves to defeat His enemies. Darkness is pushed back and evil restrained when light has gone forth through the songs of the people of the Lord.

I will never forget seeing this demonstrated before my very eyes one day three years ago at IHOPKC. At the time, I led a weekly ministry team formed to pray for healing for people struggling with critical or chronic physical illnesses.

That particular morning, we were praying with a young woman with a chronic condition. She came in doubled over with excruciating pain. Her body was swollen, and she could not even sit in a chair comfortably.

We prayed over this woman for about an hour in one of the small side-rooms in the prayer room. Though the room is closed in by a door, you can clearly hear the worship and intercession going on in the prayer room. Suddenly, one of the prophetic singers onstage began to sing an oracle she was hearing from the Lord. She sang a short prophetic song about the Lord hearing the cry of His children and answering with restoration.

After the oracle from the stage, the young woman in our room opened her eyes, and her face began to light up. Overwhelmed, she began to tell us how she felt the Lord touching her body, and she began to demonstrate how her body had shifted in those few minutes. Her swelling was gone, and her pain had completely lifted. Though she had come in barely able to walk, she left in strength and rejoiced in her healing. The Lord had moved powerfully through the simple song the singer had obediently sung that day. May we *never* discount the weak, seemingly insignificant prayers we offer before the Lord.

OUR HEARTS ARE CHANGED

The third truth that steadies my heart in the place of singing in the house of the Lord is that as I am faithful to sing His Word, He will change my heart. In each worship set, no matter if I'm feeling moved by the worship or not, if I will open my mouth and declare His Word, He will write it deep in my inner man, forming me more into His likeness. Moment by moment, this is imperceptible. Because we typically do not notice the changes, we can become discouraged with the thought that our hard hearts will never change. But over time, the knowledge of God is written on the DNA of our spirits, and we will never be the same. This is an overwhelming blessing from the Lord. We simply remain faithful day after day, and He gives life deep in our spirits.

Just as when we eat hearty, nutritious meals our bodies are strengthened, so our spirits are enlarged and strengthened as we regularly take the Word into our beings. Deuteronomy 8:3 illustrates this: "Man shall not live by bread alone; but man lives by every word that proceeds from the mouth of the Lord." Bread gives life to the body, but the Word of God releases eternal life to the soul.

The Holy Spirit promises, "This is the covenant that I will make with them . . . I will put My laws into their hearts, and in their minds I will write them" (Heb. 10:16). As we sing the Word day after day, the Lord writes His Word upon our minds, giving us understanding in the Word that releases living revelation in our lives. He writes it upon our hearts by touching our emotions and desires until they align with His holiness. We are merely responsible to open up our hearts to His activity and sing the Word of God.

Psalm 19:7–8 tells us, "The law of the Lord is perfect, *converting the soul;* the testimony of the Lord is sure, making wise the simple; the statutes of the Lord are right, rejoicing the heart; the commandment of the Lord is pure, enlightening the eyes" (emphasis added). One can never remain stagnant when he has encountered the Word of God at the heart level. If we take our roles as prophetic singers seriously, then we *constantly* connect with and minister through Scripture. The shifting I have seen in my own heart from being immersed in the Word has come as a most valued and surprising treasure. Though I loved Jesus and served Him long before I began ministering as a prophetic singer, I am a different person than I was before I began to regularly sing the Word of God. It has a tremendous transforming effect.

9

Singing the Word

As prophetic singers, our job description is to sing the Word. This requires us to be knowledgeable of the Word. If we do not know the Word, *we have nothing to sing*. The Lord takes the role of a prophetic singer seriously. Included in His invitation to function before Him as a singer is the summons to an enduring commitment to His Word. If you accept your calling as a prophetic singer, the Word of God and your call to it will rearrange your life's value system and schedule.

The Bible is the most valued resource to a prophetic singer. It is the brick and mortar of what we do, and uncovering its treasures is our highest priority. We should take note that one of the greatest prophetic singers of all time, King David, wrote song after song about the Word. We must join him in proclaiming, "I have rejoiced in the way of Your testimonies, as much as in all riches. I will meditate on Your precepts, and contemplate Your ways. I will delight myself in Your statutes; I will not forget Your word" (Ps. 119:14–16).

As we desire greater leadership anointing, ability to prophesy, and impact, we must take upon ourselves the orders the Lord gave to Joshua as he was put into leadership over the nation of Israel. The Lord said, "This Book of the Law shall not depart from your mouth, but you shall meditate in it day and night" (Josh. 1:8). His Word needs to become our meditation, day in and day out. Only then can we begin to prophesy—to sing the Word. Many mistakenly believe that prophesying means saying something made up in the moment—something fresh and never before heard. No, prophecy is birthed from and rooted in Scripture.

The Bible itself is a prophetic book, and the Holy Spirit loves every word in it. We could never come up with something better or more anointed than what He breathes on in that Book. Our job as prophetic singers is to gain an understanding of the Word, know it in our hearts, live it in our lives, and open our mouths to sing it. The Holy Spirit then anoints it with His power, and lives are changed; things are shifted in the spirit as we sing.

The Holy Spirit draws upon the knowledge of God He has formed in us as we give ourselves to be filled with the Word. I picture us as little libraries of His Word, having its many books hidden in our hearts. What we have downloaded into our hearts and minds is what the Holy Spirit has to work with when we prophesy. The more we have stored within us, the more useful we are as messengers of the Lord. This is a glorious aspect of our partnership with God.

Beautiful singing and poetic language are absolutely empty unless they are filled up with the substance of Scripture. I used to think that, since I have never been the hard-core studying type, I could just open up my heart and sing from experience. Following this line of thinking ends in our singing mostly sentiment and singing just a few phrases over and over with nowhere else to go. This is not bad or *wrong*; in fact, it is where we will all start our journey as prophetic singers. However, we *must* develop and mature in revelation. This is a valid starting place, but it is not an okay long-term mindset. We have to shake ourselves from the dust and commit to doing what it takes to grow in the understanding of His Word.

I remember years ago, I was complaining to the prayer leader of the team that I just did not know what to sing. I wanted to participate, but I had *nothing* to add. It was as though the worship cycle would begin and my mind went blank! She assured me that, if I continued to labor in the Word, in no time I would have more to sing than there was opportunity to sing it. I hoped she was right, but I couldn't imagine that I would *ever* be overflowing with things to sing.

If you feel this same discouragement as a singer, take heart. Commit yourself to pursuing the knowledge of God in the Word and begin the journey of growth so many prophetic singers have traveled before you. You may begin disheartened, but if you persist in the way, you will find you are on the path to great satisfaction and rich fulfillment in the Word.

JUST STARTING OUT

The first step to growing in knowledge of the Word is to put reading and meditating upon it in your schedule. Don't assume that because this is a priority in your heart that it will happen naturally. You must stare at how you are currently spending your time and intentionally set aside times throughout the week dedicated to reading the Bible.

Secondly, get a game plan. Map out how you will spend the time you have allotted to the study of the Word. I recommend including time simply reading through large portions of text, time in meditation, and time in detailed study. We will look at these methods individually.

READING LARGE PASSAGES

This particular form of study greatly impacted my singing during worship sets. I would say this is what most helped me cross over the barrier of not having anything to sing. I began reading large sections of Scripture by reading ten chapters of the New Testament every day. In doing this, I was reading through the whole New Testament each month.

Some follow reading plans over ninety days that include the Old Testament. The beauty of this is that it familiarizes you with the whole of Scripture. You get to step back and see the broad stroke themes the Holy Spirit is emphasizing through the Word. Related verses that you may not have spotted when seeing them in isolation begin to align since you are encountering them together in such a short period of time.

When reading large portions of Scripture at once, do not worry if you do not fully understand something—just move on. You will reencounter that verse in a month anyway, and you will be surprised about how much more sense it will make after another read-through of the entire Testament. At the same time, if your heart is drawn into a certain verse and the Lord is speaking to you, then take the time right then and there to wait on Him in meditation on that verse.

After only three months of this practice, I began to see real, tangible fruit. It was through this strategy that I began to see what my prayer leader friend had assured me of—the dots were beginning to connect, and I was finding I had more and more biblical language to sing.

MEDITATION

Meditation is a slow, prayerful way to read the Bible. The goal here is not the length of Scripture you will read; it is the *depth*. Begin your time of meditation by focusing your attention on the Holy Spirit who lives inside you (see Jn. 7:38–39; Eph. 1:13; 1 Cor. 3:16). He is your escort into the Word! He has been sent to teach you all things, and He will remind your heart of all Jesus has spoken (Jn. 14:26).

Start with a short verse or even phrase. Begin *slowly* praying through the scripture. There may be moments that you feel the presence of the Holy Spirit very strongly; allow yourself to just sit and enjoy Him before you move on in praying the verse. Let Him speak to you about His heart regarding the text. Do not get in a hurry; your purpose is not to accumulate knowledge right now. There are no rules except to open your heart and let the Lord move in you as He wills. Feel free to sit in stillness, pace, speak aloud—whatever helps you to connect with Him and slow down. Many people find it easiest to dial down within by sitting in silence.

Meditation leads to deep encounter with the Lord and results in our hearts being changed into His likeness. You may be tempted to skip this method because of the time and patience it takes, but it is in the shifting of our hearts and mindsets through meditation that there is power behind what we sing. We can sing about the love of God a thousand times, but when we have personally encountered the deep, deep love of Jesus in the Word, there comes an anointing on the words we are singing. We gain spiritual authority in the area in which we have gained personal experience. For example, when you have gained freedom from shame in your life, there is an increased anointing as you sing out biblical truths to free the shame-filled heart. A person struggling with shame can sing these same truths, but the breakthrough anointing comes on her song when she herself has received freedom. The same words of truth then carry deeper meaning from experience and greater authority. This is the difference between head knowledge and living understanding.

Do not stop singing the things you do not understand or grasp on a personal level; continue to sing the truth in faith and set aside times of meditation on Scriptures that illustrate those points. You will begin to discover a new level of authority in singing those truths as they are worked into your heart in a real way.

STUDYING THE WORD

In studying the Word, first select a passage. One simple way to go about this is to choose a whole book of the Bible at a time. It may be most impacting for you to choose a book your worship team has been singing a passage from. Gather some materials to help you: two different commentaries on that book, a set of highlighters, a pen, and some blank paper. Work your way through the book of the Bible a paragraph at a time, reading what the commentaries have to say about that segment as you go. Highlight things in the commentaries that aid you in understanding the passage. Write on the extra paper insights you receive from the commentaries or things that strike your heart as you are working your way through the passage.

It can also be helpful to cross-reference other verses as you move through the passage. Look them up and write out the helpful ones. Use these cross-references to create a paraphrase of the verses you are focusing on. You truly know a passage when you can put it in your own language while preserving the meaning of the text.

Again, there is no wrong and right way to do this. When a truth connects with your heart, take out your journal and turn what you just learned into a dialogue with the Lord. You might turn some of your study time into meditation.

Something Mike Bickle teaches regarding studying and praying the Word is that when you come across a command, speak it to the Lord, out loud or softly under your breath, and commit to following this command. Then ask Him for His help to obey it. When you come across a promise, thank Him for it and ask Him to bring it forth in your life. In this simple way, you will begin dialoguing with the Lord using the Word. The Lord intends His Word to be at the center of our relationship with Him.

ORACLES

At IHOPKC, we make room in the worship model for oracles, or short spontaneous songs, from the singers. An oracle is typically anywhere from thirty seconds to a few minutes long and can be a song from the perspective of the worshipers to God or a song from the heart of God over His people. Both can be powerful during a worship session.

While a singer's entire oracle will probably not be word-for-word Scripture, it is imperative that spontaneous songs are rooted securely in the Word. If the prophetic song is being launched like an aircraft, the Word is like the runway as it takes off and the place it returns as it lands. I have heard many creative and beautiful expressions of spontaneous songs over the years, and the ones that the Holy Spirit uses most powerfully are those birthed and released through deep understanding of the Word.

If in your spirit you are hearing phrases of a spontaneous prophetic song you might sing during a worship set, take a moment to consider their validity. Can you find the crux of your message in the Word? Does it agree with the whole of Scripture and what you know to be God's heart from your studies of the Word? If you are not confident that the answer to these questions is yes, then do not release the song. Take the time to search out the songs and phrases you receive during worship sessions. It will not be less anointed if you wait to sing them till you are sure they are biblical. This is honoring to the Lord and the Body of Christ you serve as a prophetic singer.

That said, do not shrink back from releasing a biblically-sound prophetic word from the Lord through song. When you hear the Holy Spirit whisper a verse and message into your heart, or you sense those slight impressions of the Lord as you sing, take this as an invitation to partner with Him in shifting things in the atmosphere and blessing His people. Countless times, I have heard testimonies from individuals who were deeply moved by a spontaneous oracle released in a time of worship. Many times, the singer who released the song was feeling insecure about stepping out to sing it, but because he was faithful to sing boldly the word he received, lives were touched in a profound way.

PROPHESYING AND INTERCEDING

Prophecy and intercession are two approaches to singing the Word during a worship set or prayer meeting. These two seem very difficult to differentiate at times. In fact, we often do both simultaneously. I will focus on their differences in order to distinguish them in our minds so that we may be strengthened to do both as a part of our prophetic singing.

When we are prophesying over people, nations, or situations, we are singing God's heart and promises over them. This is a strategic tool the Lord uses to increase our faith as we proclaim His sure promises and join our hearts in deeper agreement to His desires. Time and again in Scripture, the Lord has insisted that a person prophesy directly to the dire situation before a shift takes place. In Ezekiel 37:4, the Lord instructs Ezekiel: "Prophesy to these bones, and say to them, 'O dry bones, hear the word of the Lord!'" As soon as Ezekiel speaks the Lord's words to the bones, breath enters them, and they stand to their feet. God was using Ezekiel as a vessel to accomplish His purposes to bring life out of death through prophecy.

We see this again at the resurrection of Lazarus. Jesus lifts His voice in prayer to the Father. Then He shouts into the tomb: "Lazarus, come forth!" (Jn. 11:43). Immediately, the decaying body of Lazarus is made whole. We can be as confident prophesying the Word as Jesus was calling forth life in Lazarus. What He has written in Scripture, He will accomplish.

We prophesy the promises of God through either singing from the Lord's perspective or by proclaiming what He will do. For example, if you are prophesying Isaiah 62:1 over Jerusalem from the Lord's perspective, you might sing, "Oh Jerusalem, this is My promise to you: I will not rest until your righteousness shines forth!" Here is an example of your prophesying this phrase over them from your own perspective: "Oh Jerusalem, the Lord promises over you that He will not rest until your righteousness shines forth!" Both declare the Lord's intentions over Jerusalem in agreement with His Word.

Interceding as a singer usually means we are asking the Lord for something on behalf of another. As we sing phrases and oracles in intercession, we are asking the Lord to do the things He already promised in His Word He would do. Returning to our example in Isaiah 62, we might intercede using this passage by singing, "Oh Lord, break in over Jerusalem. Do not rest until her righteousness shines!" We are taking up the cause of Jerusalem before the Lord, asking Him to do what He has already clearly declared in Scripture that He longs to do.

Both prophesying and interceding are powerful ways to minister in a worship setting. I encourage you to do both regularly. While there is not a rule about which to utilize and when, you will eventually begin to discover which approach seems more effective in different circumstances.

CONTINUALLY SING THE WORD

One way to become more comfortable and familiar with singing spontaneous songs and phrases is to do so continually in secret. It is odd that many individuals sing very little offstage. We are prophetic singers even when we are at home mopping the kitchen or driving to the airport. Lift up your voice to the Lord! Sing a new song to Him. Make up choruses and oracles from the passages you have hidden in your heart. Make the verse you are currently meditating on the verse you sing throughout the day. It will quickly be written on your heart, and you will gain greater insight. Join the lifestyle of David when he wrote, "Let my mouth be filled with Your praise and with Your glory all the day" (Ps. 71:8).

STAY THE COURSE

Do not be discouraged if at first getting yourself into the secret place and spending time in the Word are a struggle. Just like we have physical appetites, we have spiritual ones as well. It may take time for your hunger for the Word to increase. If you give it time, however, you will experience the yearning to know and experience more of God in the Word. As you stay the course like that tree planted by the streams of water, you will find what it is to "delight in the law of the Lord" (Ps. 1:2).

In season and out of season, feeling it or bored, filled up with revelation or feeling barren, still we sing the Word. We set our hearts before the bonfire of His loving presence, we open up the Book whose pages are filled with the riches of revelation, and we open our mouths to sing. As prophetic singers, this is who we are. We find our joy in the Word of God.

10

Pursuing Excellence

The pursuit of excellence in singing is godly. David said in Psalm 48:1, "Great is the Lord and greatly to be praised." Indeed, He is worthy of our best offerings. We read in Psalm 33:3 that we are to sing to the Lord a new song and "play skillfully with a shout of joy." Clearly excellence and skill are to be part of our praise and worship.

This can be a confusing subject for some because, yes, it's true that the Lord enjoys the tone-deaf song of the person on row twelve just as much as the angelic voice onstage. He loves any song of love and sincerity. But when you are called and appointed to stand as a singer before the Lord, there is a stewardship factor that comes into effect.

In Matthew 25:14–30, Jesus addresses stewardship in the parable of the talents (a talent is a coin in this case). In this parable, there is a king who gives varying amounts of talents to each of his servants. When one servant increased his five talents to ten, he was greatly rewarded with authority over more resources and called a "good and faithful servant" (v. 21). Another servant was given two talents to begin with and increased them to four. He was also duly rewarded. Then there was one man who was given one talent. He buried the coin, and at the master's return offered the one coin back to him. The master called this servant, "wicked and lazy" (v. 26). Jesus explained: "To everyone who has, more will be given, and he will have abundance; but from him who does not have, even what he has will be taken away" (v. 29).

As prophetic singers, we must posture our hearts as good stewards of our calling by faithfully increasing the abilities we naturally possess. May we never be deemed lazy by the One who has gifted and called us.

ANOINTING AND EXCELLENCE

If you have been involved with worship for several years, you have probably heard someone say, "I would rather be anointed than excellent," or "I don't care how it sounds as long as I have the presence of God in my worship." While the heart behind this statement is well-meaning, to juxtapose these two values as "anointing versus excellence" is not productive in setting godly goals. Not only do we not have to choose between these two values, but we are not supposed to.

Growing in excellence, as we have discussed, is an issue of stewardship. To pit anointing against excellence is like choosing between reaching for the presence of the Lord in your worship and being a good steward. *Both* are required of us.

That said, as we begin to look at improving our vocal skills, we must see that excellence is subjective. A beginning worship team may look to one that has been functioning for several years and see something incredibly excellent. However, the London Philharmonic Orchestra may look at that advanced worship team as extremely elementary.

We must constantly be reevaluating our goals for excellence as we grow in excellence. Singing certain styles may only seem simple to you now because you have done it enough to become excellent in that area. The reason why it may feel easier to function in the anointing of the Lord when singing over one or two chords is because you have mastered the *ability* to hear and sing in that progression. You no longer have to think about *how* you are singing it; you can sing the word of the Lord undistracted.

However, simpler chord progressions and melodies are not *more anointed* than more advanced musical expression. We must keep this distinction, or we will be tempted to never stretch ourselves and grow. The goal is not to always sing in a way we are most comfortable, but to faithfully continue in reaching for the next level of singing well until it also becomes easy and second nature. Then we look to yet another level of excellence. Instead of anointing versus excellence, let's pursue excellent singing that is anointed.

THE PRACTICALS OF GETTING STARTED

There is only one way to become a better singer, and it is through hard work anointed by prayer. As much as I wish I could give you some magical, easy piece of advice that would dramatically improve your voice just by the hearing, there is no such trick. Honestly, this is the stumbling block that I have seen trip up more singers than any other in their growth. We all want to get better, but truth be told, we usually just do not want to work hard at it.

Growing in excellence as a singer takes time, the investment of energy, and oftentimes money. As a prophetic singer, I view voice lessons as part of the gig. Yes, weekly lessons are usually expensive, and you will need to add this expense in as part of your monthly budget. When you look back after several years of applying yourself to good vocal instruction, you will see how priceless that decision was and, in comparison, how small the sacrifice.

That said, lessons without regular application and practice will likely frustrate both you and your instructor. The momentum behind vocal improvement comes in daily working the instruction you are given into your voice. It is as though in the lessons your instructor points you in the direction of great singing, and your daily practice is the movement that propels you toward reaching that goal. If you do not practice, you will not move forward.

THINGS NOT TO DO

Do not approach a vocal instructor and ask for a few lessons to "get you started in the right direction" or "brush up" on your skills. This will not help you in your journey to sing well. It takes weeks upon months, even into years, to shift your voice. Yes, you will see fruit along the way in the form of small breakthroughs, and each one makes you feel like a million bucks, but the big voice maturing breakthroughs come over the course of years. When you are tempted to be discouraged, remember such breakthroughs do come! Do not let the element of long-term time investment discourage you. Believing the myth that you can pick up a few lessons on the side and not actually invest the time and energy it takes to grow is robbing you from your potential. Do not shrink back from hard work. Do what it takes! It will be worth it.

Do not tell your vocal coach that you only want to sing one certain kind of musical style. Do not say you *only* want to learn to sing worship songs well. This has become quite pervasive in prophetic singers, and putting this forth to our instructors is like asking on the front end for our growth to be stunted. If you genuinely want to grow as a vocalist, and if you really *do* want to sing those worship songs well, you will sing many songs, styles, and genres that are not your favorite. Your voice must be stretched and challenged in many areas before you achieve the level of improvement you seek.

In wanting to start and end with contemporary Christian worship songs, you are limiting your voice and will never find the whole of your abilities. The color and layers that a mature voice carries, even when singing the simplest worship song, are formed through learning and growing in many musical styles, especially classical singing. Who knows? You may find you like it!

THE PROCESS SIMPLIFIED

Put very simply, there is a three-step process to growing in excellence. You begin with technique, and then you work technique into a song. Lastly, you learn to transfer those abilities into your prophetic singing and worship.

Technique is the "stuff" of singing. It is the nitty gritty, often boring, minutia of singing well. As you work different elements of technique into your singing, the whole of your voice will change. There is no skipping this step and still moving onward to great singing. And do not consider performing technical exercises as simply a "warm up." You may use these to warm up, but even if your voice is ready and healthy, it is still important to work these abilities.

Breathing, tone, vowel formation, singing with support, vocal onsets, vocal movement, and range are a sampling of technical basics you will visit as a singer. There are many exercises for each of these subjects designed to build them into your voice. I have yet to find a singer who *loves* technique exercises, but any dedicated singer knows there is no way around them. Decide how much time you will allot daily to improving technique and stick with it.

You should always have a song or two that you are working on perfecting. These can be anything, including jazz, show tunes, opera, etc. I strongly encourage you to always have one classical piece going. This style is perhaps the most natural expression of correct vocal technique, and it will help the transfer of the good technique you are learning from your exercises into an actual song. Be brave! Sing in another language. Singing classically is a minefield of vocal improvement. Simply by venturing out of your comfort zone you will discover tools and abilities you did not know you could attain.

The last important link of this process includes transferring this newfound ability of singing with good vocal technique in classical songs to using good technique in our worship songs and spontaneous singing during sets. This breakthrough may take some time since what comes out during worship sets is largely reactionary. If we have been singing one way our whole lives, that is what will come out when we have to sing out phrases without thinking. However, if you have been diligent to practice the simple exercises and then songs with correct technique, you are incredibly close to getting that same good vocal technique to be second nature as you sing spontaneously. With time, it will be, and your voice will reach a new level of beauty and breakthrough.

Record your worship sets if at all possible. Listen to

yourself sing occasionally so you can hear your own progress. Oftentimes singers will shy away from listening to themselves, but you will probably be surprised that you sound better than you think. On the other hand, you will notice things you are doing vocally that are not sounding quite like you thought they did. Tweak what you are doing and keep listening to recordings to mark the changes. It is important that you give yourself some grace; you do not want to approach recordings of yourself with a critical spirit. That is not agreeing with the heart of the Lord over you.

ASK FOR DIVINE HELP

Earlier in the chapter, I said the only way to improve is hard work *anointed by prayer*. This is not the obligatory "don't forget to include Jesus" platitude. This is key to growing as a singer. Ask the One who *formed* your voice to anoint you to grow and learn as a vocalist. I trace several big breakthroughs in my voice back to this prayer for help and wisdom. There is a natural delay between the instruction we are given and its actualizing in our singing. In the anointing of the Holy Spirit, the delay can lessen, and what could take years can occur in a matter of months. He is the great Teacher. Go ahead and ask Him.

LOVING GOD AND OTHERS

Setting our hearts to grow in vocal ability is a key expression of loving God and those around us. It takes the devotion of our intellect, time, and energy to grow in excellence. In taking up this challenge to do what it takes to grow, we are loving God with all our *minds*. All the mental energy, study, and practice that is required is an offering of affection, all speaking loudly to Him of His great worth. "Jesus, You are worth applying my thinking and resources to extend my abilities," is what you are saying to Him in your pursuit.

Our efforts also ascribe value to the ones we are ministering with and to. We honor the people we are leading in worship when we use every resource at our disposal to improve our ability to lead them with excellence. And we show our respect to those with whom we minister by demonstrating we take what we do seriously.

You will not regret doing what it takes to grow vocally as a prophetic singer. The hardest part is actually getting started in this reach for improvement. Set your heart to sign up for the hard work of pursuing excellence, and know that He receives this sacrifice as love.

1 1

Not Quitting

I love to speak into the lives of new prophetic singers. If nothing else, there is one piece of advice I want to set before them—don't quit! New to the community and fresh out of an internship, the "wet cement" of their hearts has just been stamped with the glory, beauty, necessity, awe-inspiring wonder, and dignity of the calling to sing in the house of the Lord. This is often combined with a fresh assurance through a prophetic word from the Lord that this is their assignment from Him in this season. Quit? Why quit?

What each new singer is soon to discover is that there is a mundaneness, even a real trouble to coming again and again, day after day, to minister in a corporate worship setting. After the initial glow wears off and the beginning zeal wanes, the real work begins. And it is *work*.

I do not mean to give off the impression that becoming a singer will end in disappointment. I count what we do as one of the most precious gifts from the Lord. I am honored and amazed that I get to stand before Him declaring His worth. I cannot think of anything I would rather do or anywhere I would rather be than with a community of believers who are dedicated to His glory and watching for His coming. However, we are still human. For every day I sit on that stage with tears in my eyes, deeply encountering the Lord, there are three where doing what I do is a constant battle against the flesh.

I feel bored, weak, prideful, frustrated, and distracted. There have been seasons where set after set I sat up there struggling to love Him when all I felt was overlooked and dispensable. The truth is, even the new singer who has entered into his calling with much favor and popularity will find himself on the back row in six months, wondering if he missed his calling in God after all. And whether you are in the "front" or in the "back," the enemy comes in at just those moments when you feel all the toil of this vocation and does his best to convince you that you would be more useful to God elsewhere, doing *anything* other than singing.

For my whole career as a prophetic singer I have been on worship teams that serve in the morning. Like, *be there at 5:30* in the morning. Anyone who has ever worked a job in the earliest shift knows that each minute at that time of the day is like an eternity. On at *least* a weekly basis for years, I have gone to bed the night before a worship set excited about joining my team and singing the heart of the Lord the next day. But when the alarm goes off at 4:45 the next morning, I lie in bed staring into the darkness, seriously weighing whether or not I was actually ever called to do what I do. *Maybe now is the time for a season change,* I consider for the thousandth time.

There is a *cost* that comes with the commitment to keeping a prayer room going; there is surrender involved in keeping the fire on the altar. Even for those who are not singing full-time as a vocation, adding hours to an already busy schedule in order to show up, engage with a worship team, and actually sing to God is an incredible sacrifice.

COSTLY SACRIFICE

In 2 Samuel 24:18–25, King David went out to a certain plot of land to make a sacrifice to the Lord. He approached the owner of the property and asked to buy the threshing floor and cattle to offer on an altar. The owner generously gave him the land and oxen for the sacrifice, but David refused. He said, "No, but I will surely buy it from you for a price; nor will I offer burnt offerings to the Lord my God with that which costs me nothing" (v. 24). David understood that the Lord is honored by the personal cost it takes to build an altar before Him. He refused to bring before the Lord a sacrifice of oxen that had no element of personal sacrifice involved.

Because the lifestyle of functioning as a prophetic singer is costly, our hearts are knit to our offering of worship in a deeper way than if the road were all ease and comfort. In embracing the difficulties and facing the challenges of daily serving the Lord through song and intercession, we are joining David in proclaiming that we will not offer to the Lord that which costs us nothing. He is worth everything to us; there is no cost too high for Him to receive songs arising from every place. There is no obstacle so great that we will not persevere under pressure to fulfill the call of the Lord as a prophetic singer. In fact, we count walking out a calling that requires perseverance as a privilege; we are daily allowed to demonstrate to Him our love.

There is another time David declared his devotion to the Lord through a costly sacrifice (2 Sam. 23:14–17). At this time in his life, David was a fugitive, hiding in a cave surrounded by Philistines. David's mighty men heard him cry out in longing for a drink from the well of Bethlehem, the place of his birth (v. 15). The three main warriors left the encampment and risked their lives, maneuvering through enemy territory in order to bring David a cup of water from this well. When given the cup of precious water, David refused to drink it. Instead, he poured it out upon the ground as an offering to the Lord (v. 16).

This may initially look like foolishness. A cup of water poured upon the ground, given as a sacrifice to God? Of what use are a few ounces of water to Him? However, if we will lift our eyes for a moment from our earthly perspective and realize the magnificence and greatness of God Almighty, we will ask ourselves what good is any gift given to Him. What good are all the gold and precious treasures of earth to the One who formed the highest mountain peak with one word and measured the waters of the sea in the hollow of His hand?

Indeed, it is never the *things* we offer that are precious to the Lord; it is the heart posture behind the offering that assigns value to the gift. David understood that his mere cup of water represented the blood of his three friends who jeopardized their lives to secure it for him. It was the most costly thing he possessed, and he knew that satisfying the whim of his thirst was nowhere near worthy of the risk taken by the three warriors. As he poured it out before the Lord, he was stating that only God was worthy of such great sacrifice and devotion represented in that cup of water.

So often we want our sacrifice to God to look impressive. Moved in love for Jesus, we offer tearful declarations before Him that we would do *anything* for Him. Move to Africa as a missionary, give Him a million dollars if He would give the opportunity, stand firm in the face of martyrdom . . . *anything* to demonstrate the deep love and dedication we feel for Him. Ironically, for the vast majority of believers, the expression of love the Lord is looking for is the costliness of remaining faithful in the small and seemingly insignificant callings He has placed before us. We can get so wrapped up in looking for the next big move or change of season the Lord might bring us into that we miss His will for us in daily walking out the calling of being a prophetic singer.

There is great sacrifice in signing up again and again to

the daily difficulties of our position. No one may see all that it takes to press through the swirl of negative emotions we feel. No one else may know all it takes to work several jobs or feed three children and actually show up to the worship set on time. It may appear as inconsequential as David's few ounces of water falling to the cave floor, but the eyes of the Lord take in every amount of effort offered in love. He receives it as a valuable, worthy sacrifice.

For us, our refusal to quit through the early mornings, late nights, weariness, and temptation fills our simple song with priceless value before the Lord. We take all we have, though it looks far less grand than we envisioned, and pour it at His feet as a costly sacrifice of praise.

POSTURING OUR HEARTS FOR ENDURANCE

As we prepare to serve the Lord as singers for the long haul, we must not only be informed of the turbulence and temptation ahead, but we have to actually posture our lives in such a way that we are ready to weather the storms and come out on the other side with hearts fully abandoned to Him. In Scripture, Jesus points to Mary of Bethany as a role model for the heart that lives in a place of steady dedication. Twice it is recorded that He was moved by her love (Lk. 10:38–42; Jn. 12:1–8), and the Holy Spirit has for centuries been inviting others to emulate the posture of her heart.

In Luke 10:38–42, Jesus visited the home of the sisters,

Martha and Mary. Martha is described as being "distracted with much serving" (v. 40) and Mary as the one who "sat at Jesus' feet and heard His word" (v. 39). When Martha complained that Jesus had not rebuked Mary for neglecting to help her with the work, Jesus gently answered her: "One thing is needed, and Mary has chosen that good part, which will not be taken away from her" (v. 42).

As prophetic singers, we have to repeatedly choose the "good part" of abiding at Jesus' feet. In all our good intentions, we can easily become distracted by the work of serving Him just to realize that we are busy at the loss of actually being *with* Him.

There is only one thing truly needed, and that is to remain steadfast in the place of fellowship with our Beloved—to be where He is and do what He is doing. It is in this posture of abiding that Mary "heard His word." She was undistracted by the peripheral, lesser things and able to let His every word sink deeply into her spirit.

Prophetic singers struggle to stay in the place where His Words are actually touching our hearts at this level. We can so easily take in the Word simply as ammunition for our singing. We gain knowledge and are able to communicate His Words through song, but we lack personal depth of revelation that we can only gain by taking the time to sit before Him and truly *hear* Him with our hearts.

The second posture Jesus drew attention to in Mary was

as one who gave everything. In John 12, Jesus was spending time in Bethany before the Passover. This was the week of His death, and He chose to spend part of it with His friends, Lazarus, Martha, and Mary.

While Jesus was sitting at the table having dinner, Mary suddenly poured a pound of spikenard, expensive and fragrant oil, over His feet, and she wiped His feet with her hair (Jn. 12:3). This oil, worth about a year's wages, would likely have been her entire inheritance, her dowry to be given her husband in marriage. It was her security for the future, probably everything she had. In pouring it on Jesus, she was stating, "You are my future now—my everything."

The disciples were indignant at such a waste of money and rebuked her (v. 5). They reacted, saying in essence, "So much could have been done with the cost of this oil! What a waste!" If this sharp criticism does not sound familiar to you yet, it probably will soon. Prophetic singers and musicians who give their lives to the calling of night-and-day worship often face this same rebuke, even from other followers of Christ who misunderstand the calling of serving the Lord in worship. We hear, "What a waste of time," or "There are so many other things you could be doing for the kingdom." In the face of this accusation, we would be wise to follow the lead of Mary. She was silent. She did not cower to demands placed upon her, and she did not qualify her choices. She kept her eyes fixed on Jesus. In response, Jesus Himself thundered over her sacrifice to *leave her alone* (vv. 7–8). He took up her cause and vindicated the wisdom of her sacrifice. He validated her action as a beautiful anointing on the week of His burial.

As singers, let us look to Jesus' young friend and join her as she demonstrates the first commandment to "love the Lord your God with all your heart, with all your soul, and with all your mind" (Mt. 22:37). We touch Jesus' heart as we set our hearts to give Him *everything* we are. He is moved when we anoint Him with our song brought in loving abandon. And just as Mary truly heard His words and recognized that the hour of His death had come, so we peer into His heart and offer to Him our love in the days preceding His return.

In light of the glorious company we have in David and Mary as we give all we are to the Lord, I offer you again the advice that was given me when I first began worship leading years ago— don't quit. Don't quit when you feel like quitting, don't quit when circumstances make you feel you should quit, and don't quit when others tell you to it's time to quit—*do not quit!*

In each season of glory and trial as a singer, you are numbered among thousands of prophetic singers worldwide who are facing the same circumstances that you are. Oh that we would persevere, press into the grace of the Lord, and see the incense of worship arise to Jesus from every people, tongue, and nation. Orchestrated by the Spirit, we are prophetic singers in every place, lifting our voices in a grand symphony of praise, crying out, "Even so, Lord, come!"

SONGS OF HIS FAITHFULNESS

Full-length album

AnnaBlanc.com or iTunes

FOR I WAS FAR

New single from Anna Blanc

Get it at AnnaBlanc.com